TWENTIETH CENTURY INTERPRETATIONS OF
ABSALOM, ABSALOM!

A Collection of Critical Essays

Edited by
ARNOLD GOLDMAN

Prentice-Hall, Inc. *Englewood Cliffs, N. J.*

A SPECTRUM BOOK

Quotations from *Absalom, Absalom!* by William Faulkner (New York: Random House, Inc., 1936), copyright 1936 by William Faulkner, renewed 1964 by Estelle Faulkner and Jill Faulkner Summers, are used by permission of Random House, Inc.

The editor is grateful to Mick Gidley for sharing his knowledge and opinions of Faulkner criticism.

10 9 8 7 6 5 4 3 2 1

PRENTICE-HALL INTERNATIONAL, INC. (*London*)
PRENTICE-HALL OF AUSTRALIA, PTY. LTD. (*Sydney*)
PRENTICE-HALL OF CANADA, LTD. (*Toronto*)
PRENTICE-HALL OF INDIA PRIVATE LIMITED (*New Delhi*)
PRENTICE-HALL OF JAPAN, INC. (*Tokyo*)

Contents

TWENTIETH CENTURY
INTERPRETATIONS
OF
ABSALOM, ABSALOM!

Introduction

by Arnold Goldman

In 1902, when William Faulkner was five, his family moved to Oxford, Mississippi. There he grew up. After the First World War, during which he trained in the RAF in Canada, and a brief period as a student at the University of Mississippi, Faulkner lived for a while in New York and in New Orleans, but he returned to Oxford around the time of a momentous personal discovery about his literary talent.

> Beginning with *Sartoris* [published in 1929] I discovered that my own little postage stamp of native soil was worth writing about and that I would never live long enough to exhaust it, and that by sublimating the actual into the apocryphal I would have complete liberty to use whatever talent I might have to its absolute top. It opened up a gold mine of other people, so I created a cosmos of my own.

For an American writer to have made such a "discovery," particularly with such gusto, may seem less startling now than in 1929. Like W. B. Yeats's decision to make Irish rather than English legend and history the matter of his poetry, Faulkner's act appeared a deliberate severance from what many considered the main sources and energies of national cultural life. In 1920, H. L. Mencken had commented acidly on the "vacuity" of existence in the American South, "almost as sterile, artistically, intellectually, culturally, as the Sahara Desert." There was, he averred, a "unanimous torpor and doltishness," a "curious and almost pathological estrangement from everything that makes for a civilized culture." Except for James Branch Cabell, Mencken wrote, "you will not find a single southern prose writer who can actually write." Why, except in perverse self-stultification, would an author choose deliberately to cast his lot with "such complete sterility, so depressing a lack of all civilized gesture and aspiration?" [1]

Mencken's attack precipitated some direct attempts to reinvigorate the Southern cultural soil, including the founding of the magazine *The Double Dealer* in New Orleans, to which Faulkner contributed.[2]

---

[1] Quotations from Mencken are taken from "The Sahara of the Bozart," in *Prejudices: Second Series* (New York: Alfred A. Knopf, Inc., 1920).

[2] See William Faulkner, *New Orleans Sketches*, ed. Carvel Collins. (Rutgers: Rutgers University Press, 1958).

Another group of Southern writers, calling their magazine *The Fugitive,* congratulated themselves after one year of successful publication with having found some "oases" in the Southern Sahara. "The Fugitives," as they came to be called, and the wider group of Southern "Agrarians," however, saw all of the "industrial plutocracy" of modern American falling under Mencken's criticisms and only the South he had castigated so severely as a possible place of refuge.[3]

Though not commonly associated with any one "school" of Southern writers, Faulkner shared with the Agrarians and others a central interest in the history and significance of the region. He created, in a series of novels and stories beginning with *Sartoris* and *The Sound and the Fury* (1929), an entire section of Mississippi which he called, after an actual river, Yoknapatawpha County. In each work Faulkner searched the subject matter of the South for its qualities, for the felt life of its inhabitants, for the truth of a "glorious" past and the crippling nostalgia in its upholders. He pursued with equal intensity the "burden" of the South's history and the possibility of what historians have called "a usable past," a thread of positive tradition which could inspirit the present.

Often Faulkner depicts the dissolution of a family—the Compsons in *The Sound and the Fury,* the Sartorises in *Sartoris.* Individual members of the family struggle against what seems to them their appointed fate, defying traditions acquiesced in by those about them. Some persevere in their defiance, others succumb. Their predicaments involve both the course of wider Southern history and what Faulkner was later to call "the human heart in conflict with itself." In his imaginary county he had discovered the particular in the general, the symbolic in the actual.

In his story "An Odor of Verbena," first published in *The Unvanquished* (1938), Faulkner describes the struggle of Bayard Sartoris in the time just after the Civil War to avoid participation in an ethos of violence and revenge some would call the Southern "code of honor." Bayard's father, Colonel John Sartoris, once a prime exponent of that code, has been shot, and the community, including his stepmother, expects his son to face the killer in a gun duel. Bayard, who later defies or transmutes this tradition by confronting the assassin unarmed, recalls an earlier time, when he had already begun to see alternatives to his father's code and center them about the character of a man "whom father never forgave":

[3] See their famous manifesto *I'll Take My Stand* (New York: Harper & Brothers, 1930). Leading figures in the movement included Donald Davidson, Allen Tate and John Crowe Ransom. A short summary of their position can be found in W. J. Cash, *The Mind of the South* (1941) ch. 3, sec. 11. A general survey of the movement is John L. Stewart, *The Burden of Time* (Princeton: Princeton University Press, 1965).

"But nobody could have more of a dream than Colonel Sutpen," I said. He had been Father's second-in-command in the first regiment and had been elected colonel when the regiment deposed Father after Second Manassas, and it was Sutpen and not the regiment whom father never forgave. He was underbred, a cold ruthless man who had come into the country about thirty years before the War, nobody knew from where except Father said you could look at him and know he would not dare to tell. He had got some land and nobody knew how he did that either, and he got money from somewhere—Father said they all believed he robbed steam-boats, either as a card sharper or as an out-and-out high-wayman—and built a big house and married and set up as a gentleman. Then he lost everything in the War like everybody else, all hope of descendants too (his son killed his daughter's fiancée on the eve of the wedding and vanished) yet he came back home and set out single-handed to rebuild his plantation. He had no friends to borrow from and he had nobody to leave it to and he was past sixty years old, yet he set out to re-build his place like it used to be; they told how he was too busy to bother with politics or anything; how when Father and the other men organized the nightriders to keep the carpet-baggers from organizing the Negroes into an insurrection, he refused to have anything to do with it. Father stopped hating him long enough to ride out to see Sutpen himself and he (Sutpen) came to the door with a lamp and did not even invite them to come in and discuss it; Father said, "Are you with us or against us?" and he said, "I'm for my land. If every man of you would rehabilitate his own land, the country will take care of itself" and Father challenged him to bring the lamp out and set it on a stump where they could both see to shoot and Sutpen would not. "Nobody could have more of a dream than that."

In *Absalom, Absalom!* (1936), we see Faulkner "sublimating the actual into the apocryphal" by lodging the search for the inner mean-ing of the tragedy of the Sutpen family in the narratives of various characters. Some are Sutpen's contemporaries, some more nearly ours. Each has his own sources of information, his own biases, and his own imaginative vision. Miss Rosa Coldfield, Sutpen's sister-in-law, pic-tures him as a "demon." To her, an inherent malice lies at the heart of his efforts to establish his lineage on the hundred-square-mile Mis-sissippi plantation. To young Quentin Compson at one point in the novel, having heard the history of Sutpen from his father—who heard it from *his* father—"Sutpen's trouble was innocence" (220). Interpreta-tion is layered upon interpretation as we progress through the novel. Each time a character attempts to pluck out the heart of the mystery— what drove Sutpen on? why did his son kill his daughter's financée? —new difficulties arise:

> "It's just incredible [says Mr. Compson to Quentin]. It just does not ex-plain. Or perhaps that's it: they don't explain and we are not supposed

to know. We have a few old mouth-to-mouth tales; we exhume from old
trunks and boxes and drawers letters without salutation or signature, in
which men and women who once lived and breathed are now merely
initials or nicknames out of some now incomprehensible affection which
sound to us like Sanskrit or Chocktaw; we see dimly people, the people
in whose living blood and seed we ourselves lay dormant and waiting,
in this shadowy attenuation of time possessing now heroic proportions,
performing their acts of simple passion and simple violence, impervious
to time and inexplicable. . . . They are there, yet something is missing;
they are like a chemical formula exhumed along with the letters from
that forgotten chest, carefully, the paper old and faded and falling to
pieces, the writing faded, almost indecipherable, yet meaningful, familiar
in shape and sense, the name and presence of volatile and sentient forces;
you bring them together in the proportions called for, but nothing happens; you re-read, tedious and intent, poring, making sure that you have
forgotten nothing, made no miscalculation; you bring them together
again and again nothing happens: just the words, the symbols, the
shapes themselves, shadowy inscrutable and serene, against the turgid
background of a horrible and bloody mischancing of human affairs."
(100–101)

Mr. Compson's fatalistic acquiescence in the insolubility of the
puzzle is unacceptable to Quentin, whom Faulkner's readers would
already have met as the Harvard-attending brother in *The Sound and
the Fury*. In that novel a whole chapter chronicles the day upon which
he commits suicide by drowning himself in the Charles River rather
than return south to face the growing disintegration of his own
family. In *Absalom, Absalom!*, Quentin's involvement with the Sutpens is placed in the previous summer (1909), when he hears their
history from his father and from Rosa Coldfield and accompanies her
to the derelict Sutpen mansion. In January (1910), on receipt of a
letter from his father describing the burning of the old Sutpen mansion and the death of Miss Coldfield, Quentin and his Harvard roommate Shreve converse deep into the night in a final exhausting effort to
wring the truth about the Sutpens from the many confusing and conflicting reports.[4]

About the ultimate "truth" of Sutpen and his children's motives and
actions there is still critical dispute.[5] There is likewise little unanimity
but much helpfulness in various critics' attempts to tell us what *kind*
of novel *Absalom, Absalom!* is. For some it is "gothic" in form, both
in the melodrama of its events and the multiplicity of second- and

[4] Cleanth Brooks's careful tabulation (reprinted below pp. 107–13) shows clearly on
what sources Quentin and Shreve base their conception and just how much of it is
wholly speculative.

[5] See Richard P. Adams, *Faulkner: Myth and Motion* (Princeton, N.J.: Princeton
University Press, 1968), pp. 198–99 for a criticism of Brooks's view.

third-hand narrations.[6] Thus it can be related, as does Michael Millgate (see below, pp. 55–57), to Emily Brontë's *Wuthering Heights* and Charlotte Brontë's *Jane Eyre*. Others see the mythic character of its familiar plot and consider *Absalom, Absalom!* a prose tragedy.[7] It also has many of the attributes of the historical novel. As described by G. R. Stange,

> The serious historical novel . . . expresses a theory of history. Whatever its particular subject, it is designed to illustrate the necessary connections between the individual life and the social order, to arrive at a coherent interpretation of a significant moment of the past. In such a novel the main characters are often both individuals and representatives of historical tendencies. . . .
>
> The period that a historical novelist chooses to study is usually one of crisis; it is in the nature of his interest that he should want to explore a moment in which great forces come into open conflict. . . . The period of Thackeray's *Henry Esmond* is one in which an old order is destroyed and a new polity created; Thackeray's great event is The Glorious Revolution. . . . Esmond is the kind of character he is because he is conceived as the representative of a new social type. It is essential to the narrative that Esmond should be in the middle of the historical conflict, open to pressure from both sides.[8]

Sutpen, compared to the more established Colonel Sartoris and General Compson, is a "new man." [9] He had come "out of no discernable past and acquired his land no one knew how and built his house, his mansion apparently out of nothing" (11). Between 1833, when he arrives in Yoknapatawpha County (31–34) and the Civil War, Sutpen becomes "the biggest single landowner and cotton-planter in the county" (72).

On two occasions, according to Quentin, Sutpen discussed his "design" with Quentin's grandfather. In 1835, he revealed his past—how he had been born in West Virginia,

---

[6] See, e.g., Irving Howe, *Faulkner: A Critical Study*, revised edition (New York: Vintage Books, 1962), pp. 71–78 and Malcolm Cowley's review in *The New Republic*, November 4, 1936, p. 22, titled "Poe in Mississippi."

[7] See Richard Sewell, *The Vision of Tragedy* (New Haven and London: Yale University Press, 1959), pp. 133–47, and John Paterson, below pp. 34–41.

[8] G. Robert Strange, "Introduction" to William Makepeace Thackeray, *The History of Henry Esmond, Esq.* (New York: Holt, Rinehart and Winston, Inc., 1962), pp. xv–xvii. See also Georg Lukács, *The Historical Novel*, tr. Hannah and Stanley Mitchell (Harmondsworth, England: Penguin Books, 1969), chap. 1.

[9] In *Requiem for a Nun* (1951) Faulkner wrote that Sutpen's arrival in Jefferson, Mississippi, had, in fact, preceded that of John Sartoris. Sutpen was, however, regarded as an interloper by families who felt their own "aristocratic" pretensions. For a description of these new men see Ward L. Miner, *The World of William Faulkner* (New York: Pageant Book Co., 1959) pp. 29, 48. Melvin Backman's essay, reprinted below pp. 59–75, is also relevant.

"where the only colored people were Indians and you only looked down at them over your rifle sights, where he had never even heard of, never imagined, a place, a land divided neatly up and actually owned by men who did nothing but ride over it on fine horses or sit in fine clothes on the galleries of big houses while other people worked for them. . . . Because where he lived the land belonged to anybody and everybody and so the man who would go to the trouble and work to fence off a piece of it and say 'This is mine' was crazy. . . . So he didn't even know there was a country all divided and fixed and neat with a people living on it all divided and fixed and neat because of what colour their skins happened to be and what they happened to own, and where a certain few men not only had the power of life and death and barter and sale over others, but they had living human men to perform the endless repetitive personal offices, such as pouring the very whisky from the jug and putting the glass into a man's hand or pulling off his boots for him to go to bed. . . ." (221–22)

Sutpen's family drift eastward, into Tidewater Virginia, and one day when Thomas is about thirteen, a momentous event occurs—he is turned away from the front door of a plantation house ("the biggest house he had ever seen") by a house slave ("the monkey-dressed nigger butler"). The affront seems so great to the boy, so overwhelmed is he by the vision of his nonentity in this strange new world, that he determines then and there, that

" 'to combat them you have got to have what they have that made them do what the man did. You got to have land and niggers and a fine house to combat them with.' " (238)

He leaves home and goes to Haiti, where he manages a plantation, puts down a slave uprising, and marries. He also tells Quentin's grandfather "how he had put his first wife aside": " 'I found that she was not and could never be, through no fault of her own, adjunctive or incremental to the design which I had in mind' " (240). He provides for her and their child and two years later appears in Yoknapatawpha County to begin his career as a Mississippi plantation-owner.

For years the "design" flourishes. Sutpen marries Ellen Coldfield, a storekeeper's daughter, and faces down the hostility of the townspeople of Jefferson to his strange and solitary ways. Two children are born, Henry in 1839 and Judith in 1841. All seems in order for the establishment of a family dynasty, a complete success story in getting back at the world of aristocratic power and prestige by joining and even outdoing it. But in 1860, just as a specter threatens the continuance of that social order, and everyone admits "that war was inevitable,"

the destiny of Sutpen's family which for twenty years now had been like a lake welling from quiet springs into a quiet valley and spreading, rising almost imperceptibly and in which the four members of it floated in sunny suspension, felt the first subterranean movement toward the outlet, the gorge which would be the land's catastrophe too. . . . (74)

Soon his daughter Judith has become engaged to his son's college classmate, Charles Bon; Sutpen has mysteriously forbidden the marriage; and Henry has left home, apparently self-disinherited. The coming of the Civil War holds this unlooked-for hindrance to the completion of Sutpen's "design" in suspension, though by 1864, when a Southern defeat has become likely, Sutpen himself feels "old" and sees "time shortening ahead of him" (261). A second time he explains himself to General Compson:

> " 'You see, I had a design in my mind. Whether it was a good or a bad design is beside the point; the question is, Where did I make the mistake in it, what did I do or misdo in it, whom or what injure by it to the extent which this would indicate. I had a design. To accomplish it I should require money, a house, a plantation, slaves, a family—incidentally of course, a wife. I set out to acquire these, asking no favor of any man.' " (263)

He explains at length how he "repudiated" his first wife because of "one fact" which was "withheld" from him, a "new fact [which] rendered it impossible that this woman and child be incorporated in my design" (264). He feels that he acted according to strict principle in providing for her—so he cannot understand where his plan went wrong. We realize that his present perplexity has something to do with this act.

Earlier in the novel, Quentin's father speculates at length as to why Sutpen had forbidden the marriage of his daughter Judith and Charles Bon. He thinks it was because Bon, from New Orleans, had an octoroon mistress, or that he would not give the mistress up. After Quentin has visited the derelict Sutpen mansion in September, 1909, however, he appears to know that Charles Bon was Sutpen's son by his "repudiated" first wife. Thus Sutpen is trying to prevent an incestuous union. Quentin imagines Sutpen, caught in a cleft stick, saying to General Compson,

> " 'either choice which I might make, either course which I might choose, leads to the same result: either I destroy my design with my own hand [by acknowledging Bon as his son], which will happen if I am forced to play my last trump card, or do nothing [to prevent the marriage], let matters take the course which I know they will take and see my design complete itself quite normally and naturally and successfully to the public eye, yet to my own in such fashion as to be a mockery and a betrayal of that little boy who approached that door fifty years ago and was turned away, for whose vindication the whole plan was conceived and carried forward to the moment of this choice. . . .' " (274)

Though Henry Sutpen apparently takes Charles Bon's side when the marriage is forbidden, he shoots Bon at the gate of the Sutpen mansion just as the Southern cause itself is collapsing in defeat. Discussing his motivation, Quentin and Shreve feel that Henry could even have accepted the idea of incest, casting aside "all the voices of his heredity and training which said *No. No. You cannot. You must not. You shall not*" (342–43). Carried even further by the compelling mystery of the events, Quentin and Shreve's separate voices fuse: though they are talking far into the night in a Harvard room in 1910,

> They were both in Carolina and the time was forty-six years ago, and it was not even four now but compounded still further, since now both of them were Henry Sutpen and both of them were Bon, compounded each of both yet either neither. . . . (351)

They imagine a final interview in the last days of the War between Sutpen and his estranged son, with whom he has not spoken since Christmas, 1860. Sutpen tells Henry why Charles Bon must not marry Judith:

> —*He must not marry her, Henry. His mother's father told me that her mother had been a Spanish woman. I believed him; it was not until after he was born that I found out that his mother was part negro.* (354–55)

Thus, for Quentin and Shreve, even if Henry could accept his half-brother as a brother-in-law, he cannot accept a Negro as one, and he shoots Bon dead to prevent the marriage.

Subsequently, Sutpen becomes possessed by a desire to "restore" his lost dream. Rosa Coldfield sees him *"begin at once to salvage what was left of Sutpen's Hundred and restore it"* (154):

> *We were right about what he would intend to do: that he would not even pause for breath before undertaking to restore his house and plantation as near as possible to what it had been.* (160)

Hence we see the defiance of his neighbors' opposition to the carpetbaggers in the postwar South:

> *he refused* [to join them], *declined, offered them . . . defiance if it was defiance they wanted, telling them that if every man in the South would do as he himself was doing, would see to the restoration of his own land, the general land and South would save itself. . . .* (161)

Rosa sees him *"fighting . . . against the ponderable weight of the changed new time itself"* (162). Her animus against Sutpen is noticeable behind all her remarks to Quentin, and she reveals that during this time Sutpen proposed to her and she accepted, only to discover that he wished to see if she would produce a male heir to replace the missing Henry before they actually married. Doggedly Sutpen pursues the chimera of a design, but just when he realizes that the task of restoration is impossible, that he will have hardly one square mile, let alone one hundred, he half-provokes the poor-white Wash Jones into killing him by seducing Jones's granddaughter and callously scorning her when she gives birth to a daughter instead of the son he still wanted.[10]

A grim irony pervades this fable and marks its precise difference from the classic historical novel. Unlike the typical hero of the historical novel, Thomas Sutpen does not change with changing times. He pursues his self-appointed course to a bitter end.

> The hero . . . is usually an orphan (though he may be only spiritually orphaned); he is personally gifted, but of an ambiguous or, at any rate, not entirely secure social position; in the course of the novel he undergoes initiation, moving from innocence to experience. . . . He falls in love, usually more than once (the stereotype would be one false love and—ultimately—one true). He is devastated by a reverse of fortune, but from this suffering he learns the moral or social truth that makes it possible for him to rise and live again.[11]

This is the pattern which Sutpen attempts to fulfill, but only creates an antitype of. As he fails to gain any moral or social truth from his "reverse of fortune" ("Whether it was a good or bad design is beside the point," he says), he becomes a failed hero.

The typical hero, though originally sympathetic to the "older" cause and an older ethos, would move painfully towards a *rapprochement* with the newer, thus figuring the larger national travail itself. Just as the Civil War is, however, no Glorious Revolution bringing progress and modernity to the South, so Sutpen holds to the last to the intentions he had formed as an adolescent. He inverts the hero's role, just as the novel sees Southern history as an inversion of the model of crisis and progress enshrined in the classical historical novel of the nineteenth century.

As in *Absalom, Absalom!*, in Thomas Hardy's *The Mayor of Casterbridge* a powerful, prominent man, set in ways which are clearly being threatened by a newer, more modern outlook on the world, cannot bend and is broken. Like Sutpen he has set aside a wife (he sold her to a sailor at a fair) and in his prosperity the past returns to haunt him. John Paterson, whose essay, reprinted on pp. 32–41, compares *The Mayor of Casterbridge* with *Absalom, Absalom!*, considers them

---

[10] There is a longer version of this episode in the story "Wash," which is to be found in *The Collected Stories of William Faulkner* (1950), pp. 535–50. "Wash" was first published in *Harper's* 168 (February, 1934): 258–66, and reprinted in *Doctor Martino and Other Stories* (1934).

[11] This is Strange's description of the *Bildungsroman* hero (op. cit., pp. xx–xxi). For him, the two forms are conflated in historical novels like *Henry Esmond*.

as tragedies, but both also share most importantly this reversal of the typical pattern of the historical novel and the *Bildungsroman* forms.[12]

It is a much-debated question whether Sutpen's failure reflects upon any "moral bankruptcy" in the antebellum South itself, and indeed whether his inability to alter after the War characterizes—and even criticizes—a more general Southern response. After all, according to theorists like Georg Lukács, the specific feature which created the historical novel was "the derivation of the individuality of characters from the historical peculiarity of their age," as in the novels of Sir Walter Scott, who

> endeavours to portray the struggles and antagonisms of history by means of characters who, in their psychology and destiny, always represent social trends and historical forces.[13]

For Cleanth Brooks, however, Sutpen is less a representative of the older Southern culture than an "American," the "new man" who misunderstands and distorts the inner meaning of that culture.[14] For others, Sutpen represents the extreme form of tendencies inherent in the plantation society, and his downfall is an object-lesson in the pure mathematics of its adoption of and reliance on chattel slavery. In this view, the extent to which the South is racked by its refusal to recognize the black man as a "brother" is figured in Sutpen's and Henry's inability to recognize, let alone admit, the claim of Charles Bon. It is ironical that a social pattern which Sutpen had only accepted as a mode of "vindication," and which was not a prejudice or conviction of the inherent inferiority of the black man, has apparently been internalized in his son. Henry, who might through his association with Bon have become less the provincial Puritan and more the tolerant man-of-the-world, kills Bon not to prevent his father's "design" from being shattered, but because (according to Quentin and Shreve) the Negro is an inferior being. It is for Quentin Compson, who sought to make *sense* of the Sutpen story, a ghastly and immobilizing conclusion in which he feels implicated.

---

[12] Students of the historical novel and the *Bildungsroman* may also wish to compare *Absalom, Absalom!* with Tobias Smollett's *The Expedition of Humphrey Clinker* and Thackeray's sequel to *Henry Esmond*, *The Virginians*. In each, a central issue is whether the next generation, in the persons of two brothers (half-brothers in Smollett, twins in Thackeray) of polar character, will usher in the new era successfully or not.

[13] Lukács, op. cit., pp. 15, 33.

[14] See Cleanth Brooks, *William Faulkner: The Yoknapatawpha Country* (New Haven and London: Yale University Press, 1963), pp. 295–324. Michael Millgate's comments on Faulkner's unpublished story "The Big Shot" (see below, pp. 52–55) demonstrate that elements of this Gatsby-like character went into the creation of Thomas Sutpen. This seems to suggest that a more generally "American" emphasis was involved at some stage.

"According to Quentin and Shreve!" The very idea of a "design" pursued into a changed time, the pattern of a counterhistorical novel —must we attribute these too only to the point-of-view of characters? [15] If so, why has Faulkner, having created the convention of a multiplication of divergent views and their convergence upon Quentin Compson, gone beyond even suggesting that Quentin synthesizes these views to an amount of authorial confirmation, both in the narrative technique of the final portion of the novel and in the provision of an apparently definitive Chronology and Genealogy? It may be that neither of the simple solutions—the novel of multiple points of view and the novel which eventuates in a "true" version—is satisfactory: *Absalom, Absalom!* perpetually tempts us to validate Quentin's historiography and perpetually withholds final authorization. This tension, and its effect on the idea of a "story" is examined by James Guetti, who sees the novel's contradictions necessitated by its particular imaginative vision.[16]

It is noteworthy that Faulkner chose to set Quentin upon his quest in 1909 and 1910, the very nadir, we might think, of Southern culture as seen from the perspective of the later "renaissance." The dating effectively denies Quentin the benefit—if any—derivable from a decade and more which saw the development of various modes of dealing with the "burden" of Southern history. His efforts thus become the more poignant just as they inhibit the author from implying a definitive judgment on the possibility or impossibility of ultimate success. We cannot tell whether Quentin's discovery, to use Richard Poirier's formulation, "that man and his history are mutually hostile and alien; that he is merely the reflex of some impersonal and abstract historical process," is shared by Faulkner.[17] Quentin seems the victim as well of his very frame of reference—terms such as "history," "search," "freedom"—and Faulkner claims no special exemption from this frame: Quentin's experience shapes his fiction.

In the hopeful story, the mirror preserves the observer where direct confrontation of the Gorgon petrifies. Quentin Compson followed the Sutpens at distance, but in possessing them is possessed by them. Faulkner has accepted a like risk, and in *Absalom, Absalom!* shares even as he identifies Quentin's fate. Through him so do we.

[15] See Brooks's tabulation, Appendix B, below (pp. 107–13) and note 5, above. Some critics see the use of Quentin as a "filter" or focus an especial advantage (see Sewall, *The Vision of Tragedy*, p. 136, and Richard Poirier, below [pp. 12–15, 22]). Others think it diminishes the novel (see John Paterson, below, pp. 37–39).

[16] See Guetti, below (pp. 76–100). Guetti is extending the implications of Walter Slatoff's ideas. See Slatoff, *Quest for Failure: A Study of William Faulkner* (Ithaca, N.Y.: Cornell University Press, 1960).

[17] See Poirier, below (pp. 12–31).

"Strange Gods" in Jefferson, Mississippi:
Analysis of *Absalom, Absalom!*

by *Richard Poirier*

Almost without exception, existing criticism of Faulkner has ignored *Absalom, Absalom!* or has examined it either as a naturalistic novel full of Gothic horror and romantic attitudinizing or as little more than a curious source book, significant only for what it can tell us about the problems of Quentin Compson in *The Sound and the Fury*. The only notable exception of which I am aware is Malcolm Cowley's essay "William Faulkner's Legend of the South." [1] But the commentary on *Absalom, Absalom!* which is included in that essay is not meant by Mr. Cowley to be extensive, and it only partially succeeds, it seems to me, in suggesting the true character of the novel.

An understanding of the environment which we see conditioning Quentin in *The Sound and the Fury* is of course helpful. We can perhaps better appreciate his response to experience in *Absalom, Absalom!* if we have learned from the earlier book that Quentin's disillusionment, the vacuity of purpose which plagues him, cannot be divorced from the spiritual dead end which his mother represents and which his father pathetically articulates. The latter, summing up his view of life, tells Quentin that "Time is your misfortune." [2] The remark is characteristic of Mr. Compson's teaching throughout *The Sound and the Fury*. In terms of it, his son has been deprived of the possibility of abstracting human values from a historical context. The father has slowly undermined for Quentin the myth of any spiritual

"'Strange Gods' in Jefferson, Mississippi: Analysis of Absalom, Absalom!" by Richard Poirier. From Frederick J. Hoffman and Olga W. Vickery, eds., William Faulkner: Two Decades of Criticism (East Lansing: Michigan State University Press, 1951), pp. 217–43. Reprinted by permission of the publisher.

[1] Malcom Cowley, "William Faulkner's Legend of the South," *The Sewanee Review*, LIII (Summer, 1945), 343–61. [Subsequently revised in the Introduction to *The Portable Faulkner* (New York: The Viking Press, Inc., 1946), pp. 94–109. This Introduction has been reprinted in both Hoffman and Vickery, eds., *William Faulkner: Three Decades of Criticism*, op. cit. and Robert Penn Warren, ed., *Faulkner, A Collection of Critical Essays* (Englewood, N.J.: Prentice-Hall, Inc., 1966), pp. 34–45. Ed.]

[2] *The Sound and the Fury* (New York: Random House, 1946), p. 123.

transcendence of what seems to be the mechanism of historical fact. This is in great part the problem faced by Quentin in *Absalom, Absalom!* as well. It is a problem which makes Quentin, as an organizer of Thomas Sutpen's story, the dramatic center of this novel. Indeed, in *Absalom, Absalom!* Quentin is nearly allowed to appropriate the position of the author.

But this is not to say, as many have, that Quentin or some other character is Faulkner's spokesman. Faulkner is extremely careful to prevent his novels from ever being controlled by the "efficient confessionals" which Kenneth Burke claims to find in them.[3] The form in both *The Sound and the Fury* and *Absalom, Absalom!* prevents any one of the narrators from seducing the reader to a restricted, wholly individual point of view. It is quite clear that the author sympathizes in the earlier book with Benjy and Quentin. But if we are looking for Faulkner to express himself, we shall find that he does so impersonally in the structure of the work itself. Benjy, Quentin, and Jason tend, in different degrees, to neutralize one another. It is the structure of *The Sound and the Fury* which emphasizes the wholeness of Dilsey's point of view and which affirms the presence, if only as a choral effect, of a traditional and moral context in which we can place the whole novel.

The adaptation of this method to a new set of circumstances constitutes the most significant connection between *The Sound and the Fury* and *Absalom, Absalom!* In the formal arrangement of this later novel, for example, we see Faulkner's sense of history played off against the social irresponsibility of Rosa Coldfield, the most consciously incantatory of all his narrators. We see Thomas Sutpen try to make history begin in his own image and, when the damage is done, Quentin Compson attempt to discover the meaning of his historical background with Sutpen as the central figure. The attempt to create history is both the story of Sutpen and, with a difference, the conscious effort of Quentin as a narrator of that story. Faulkner has joined the two themes so that the persisting disruptions caused by Sutpen almost fatally affect Quentin's attempt to discover the meaning of his heritage.

Because Quentin, if he is to define himself, must confront these persisting disruptions, it is little wonder that Faulkner is so obviously fond of him. The preoccupations and the difficulties of the two are not dissimilar. Within the chaotic nature of Sutpen's history and Rosa's "demonizing," Quentin tries to find some human value adhering to what is apparently a representative anecdote of his homeland. In doing so, he must somehow overcome a problem such as confronts the contemporary writer. As T. S. Eliot defines it, it is the problem of overcoming "the damage of a lifetime and of having been born into

---

[3] Kenneth Burke, *The Philosophy of Literary Form* (Baton Rouge, 1941), p. 117.

an unsettled society." [4] And Quentin is "older at twenty," he tells
Shreve, "than a lot of people who have died" [p. 377].[5]

In Quentin's mind, the career of Thomas Sutpen is the most per-
sistently disturbing element in the history of his native region, and
one in which all of his family have been involved. Indeed, his preoccupation with the meaning of the story is so distressing that he can
see no respite from it even in the future: "Nevermore of peace. Nevermore of peace. Nevermore Nevermore Nevermore" [p. 373]. The reader
who is acquainted with *The Sound and the Fury* may understandably
wish to view Quentin's problem here in terms of his experience in
the earlier novel. Quentin cannot, for example, hear Rosa continue
the story past her recounting of the murder of Charles Bon. He may
see in this incident a distorted image of his own failure in *The Sound
and the Fury* to defend the honor of his sister, Caddy, and of the
incest which he claims to have committed. At different times Quentin
associates himself both with Bon, who feels compelled to threaten
incest, and with Henry, Judith's brother, who must kill his friend to
prevent it and the accompanying evil of miscegenation. Quentin,
who could neither dignify Caddy's immorality by the damning sin of
incest nor properly defend his sister's honor, discovers something of
himself in history by recreating the circumstances which led to Bon's
murder. But it is well to remember that Quentin's interest in Sutpen's
story transcends any reference he finds in it for such personal problems,
which, after all, we are acquainted with only from observing his activity
outside the context of *Absalom, Absalom!* Had Quentin assumed the
luxury of treating the Sutpen story merely as an objectification of some
personal obsession, the total effect of the novel would have partaken
of the overindulgent and romantic self-dramatization of Rosa's soliloquy.

Quentin tries to place Sutpen in a social and historical context. By
doing so he can perhaps discover his own tradition and the reasons for
its collapse. His father tells him that in Sutpen's day, in Quentin's
past, the circumstances in which people operated at least simplified
what Mr. Robert Penn Warren refers to as the risks of being human:[6]

of that day and time, of a dead time; people too as we are, and victims
too as we are, but victims of a different circumstance, simpler and therefore, integer for integer, larger, more heroic . . . not dwarfed and involved but distinct, uncomplex who had the gift of living once or dying
once instead of being diffused and scattered creatures . . . [p. 89].

[4] *After Strange Gods* (London, 1934), p. 54.
[5] Page references to *Absalom, Absalom!* are to the Random House edition, 1936.
[6] "Cowley's Faulkner," *The New Republic*, CXV (August 12, 1946), 177. [Re-
printed in Frederick J. Hoffman and Olga W. Vickery, eds., *William Faulkner:
Three Decades of Criticism* (New York: Harcourt, Brace & World, Inc., A Harbinger
Book, 1963), pp. 109–24. Ed.]

Quentin will discover that the times were not so "simple" as his
father imagines. But he is still painfully aware of the deprivation
his father defines, a deprivation which Shreve, who lays no claim
either on the past or to a tradition, cannot fully understand. Perhaps
Malcolm Cowley is right and the Sutpen story represents for Quentin
the essence of the Deep South.[7] But *Absalom, Absalom!* is not primarily
about the South or about a doomed family as a symbol of the South.
It is a novel about the meaning of history for Quentin Compson. The
story of Sutpen simply represents that part of the past which Quentin
must understand if he is to understand himself. In this respect, Quentin's dilemma is very similar to that of Stephen Dedalus in *Ulysses.*
Whether the scene is Ireland or the South, the problem of extracting
value from a cultural heritage remains about the same. Indeed, Quentin has his own Buck Mulligan in his roommate, Shreve McCannon.
When Shreve and other students at Harvard ask Quentin about the
South, they really demand that he justify his own existence: *Tell about
the South. What's it like there. What do they do there. Why do they
live there. Why do they live at all . . .* [p. 174]. The painful consequence of Quentin's reply—which is the story of Sutpen—is that all
of the questions remain for Shreve unanswered. Part of the history
which Quentin reconstructs is a record of violence and evil. But Quentin hopes, when he begins, that in the world in which Sutpen lived,
unlike his own world in *The Sound and the Fury,* violence was of
some moral consequence and evil was at least a violation of a corrupti-
ble but not wholly devitalized moral code.

Regardless of what Sutpen might represent in Quentin's mind, it is
soon made obvious to the reader, though the point is often missed,
that he is above all a special case. In the context of the novel he is not
even a typical Southern planter. It is emphasized that at least three of
the other characters, Wash Jones, Charles Bon, and Mr. Coldfield,
were at one time confronted respectively with the very things which
injured Sutpen: the same social antagonism, nearly the same act of
repudiation, and an almost identical opportunity to exploit the evils
of the economic system. Sutpen alone seems able to pursue his ambition, what he calls his "design," not only in defiance of an outraged
community but in ignorance of its codes and customs and with a complete insensitivity to human character.

Like the violence of Joe Christmas in *Light in August,* Sutpen's
"design" is directed as much against a terrifying sense of his own
insufficiency as against a society which apparently standardizes that
insufficiency by caste or class systems. When his family moves from
the primitively communal society of their mountain home to settle in
the Tidewater, young Sutpen finds everything in the new environment

[7] Cowley, *Sewanee Review,* LIII (Summer, 1945), 344.

phenomenal: the Negroes, the social customs, the differences in living standards among the white men employed, like his father, on the plantation. The boy cannot understand how or why this place should differ from the mountain settlement where "the land belonged to anybody and everybody" [p. 221]. He is naturally humiliated and confused when, carrying a message to the plantation owner, he is ordered away from the front door by a Negro in livery. Because he has been brought up in a society outside the one in which he now lives, he cannot fit the action of the "monkey nigger" into any acknowledged social pattern. It can be seen by young Sutpen only as a wholly personal affront. At the door, he finds himself "looking out from within the balloon face" of the Negro [p. 234], and at himself. Having no past, no background of his own by which he could appreciate the social complexity of the incident, he prejudicially assumes the position of his insulter, or the agent of his insulter, and both pities and degrades himself. At first he considers immediate revenge: he will shoot the Negro and the owner of the house. But he finally decides that the best thing he can do is to become as rich and powerful as the man from whose door he has been turned. This ambition develops into what he later calls his "design."

When Sutpen tells Quentin's grandfather about this incident, he claims that he felt then that "he would have to do something about it in order to live with himself for the rest of his life" [p. 234]. Years later he explains to General Compson that the "design" was "not what he wanted to do but what he just had to do, had to do it whether he wanted to or not" [p. 220]. He justifies himself by an appeal not to any moral code which might have been violated at the plantation door, but to some inexplicable compulsion over which he apparently can exert no discipline. It might be argued that Sutpen makes the worst of what someone like Wash Jones would have assimilated into the accepted order of things. In any case, the rest of his life is dedicated to a vindication of that little boy at the door, what he himself calls "the boy symbol" [p. 261].

The "boy symbol" motif persists throughout the novel and becomes connected with Sutpen's desire for a son. Indeed, the whole "design" is a calculated bid for a kind of immortality. His son and the rest of his descendants shall have all Sutpen lacked: wealth, power, untainted respectability. To that end, he first goes to Haiti to make a fortune only to abandon it and to repudiate his first wife and son, Charles Bon, when he discovers that she has a trace of Negro blood. The hundred-square-mile plantation called Sutpen's Hundred which he later builds in Mississippi is really a second and, it seems, unassailable foundation of the power and wealth that his heir, Henry Sutpen, shall perpetuate. And for respectability he chooses, much to the town's indignation, Ellen Coldfield, daughter not of the richest but of the most primly respectable and most religious family in Jefferson. It is characteristic of Sutpen that in selecting his wife he chooses, in place of the aristocratic connection he wishes to make, a marriage into a family which is merely priggishly proud. Without any sense or knowledge of the past, Sutpen, through his son, would belong only to the future. Quentin imagines that Bon recognized Henry as his brother by seeing in his face the image of *"the man who shaped us both out of that blind chancy darkness which we call the future"* [p. 317]. As a reflection of the vindicated boy symbol, Henry becomes for his father a means of disowning the past.

When Sutpen arrived in Jefferson to upset the town first by his unorthodox and dishonest methods and then by apparently corrupting the Coldfields, he was, Rosa says, "a man who so far as anyone . . . knew, either had no past or did not dare reveal it—a man who rode into town out of nowhere" [p. 16]. It is significant that Sutpen gives a very poor account of his own experiences and that he treats his activity prior to Jefferson with boredom, almost with disinterest. Quentin's grandfather, who is really the one person in town who befriends Sutpen, manages to induce him to recount some of his past life. When Sutpen does so, it is as if he were just

> . . . telling a story about something a man named Thomas Sutpen had experienced, which would still have been the same story if the man had had no name at all, if it had been told about any man or no man over whiskey at night [p. 247].

He shows no regard whatever for cause and effect and, General Compson complains, little for logical sequence. Such an inability to tell his own story is indicative of Sutpen's refusal to believe that anyone could have any interest in his past activity. He can ignore the details of his past because, as far as he is concerned, they hold no portent of his future. In terms of his "design," he has achieved a self-identification beyond anything that has been done or can be done to him.

But ironically enough, that part of his past which he outlines for General Compson will later indicate to Quentin the source and the reasons for the retribution which overtakes him. The General himself is aware of the perilous quality of this man's calculated activity when he hears Sutpen bombastically explain the disposition of his first wife. He has dared treat her as an abstract, expendable counter to be used by him with "fairness" but with complete impersonality:

> I found that she was not and could never be, through no fault of her own, adjunctive or incremental to the design which I had in mind, so I provided for her and put her aside [p. 240].

According to Quentin, "Sutpen's trouble was 'innocence' ":

> . . . that innocence which believed that the ingredients of morality were like the ingredients of pie or cake and once you had measured them

and balanced them and mixed them and put them into the oven it was
all finished and nothing but pie or cake could come out [p. 263].

Part of that "innocence" is, of course, the belief that any woman will
accept money as a final recompense for desertion. Bon's sudden and
ironically unintentional appearance with Henry at Sutpen's Hundred
makes that expression of Sutpen's "innocence" seem purblind indeed.
Sutpen, who at least gave Bon the name he bears, is the only one in
the family who is aware of the guest's real identity. But all he can do
for the present is to remain silent. To acknowledge that Charles Bon
is his son would be to infuse humanity into the "ingredients" of his
"design." He is simply incapable of doing it. He fails to realize that
Bon is demanding only the same sort of recognition denied him as a
boy at the plantation door. And he can forget human need so completely that he cannot understand how or why his plans could be so
affected by what he calls "a maelstrom of unpredictable and unreasoning human beings" [p. 275].

Sutpen's story might well be about his opportunities for becoming
human. There are countless opportunities, like the appearance of Bon,
which he has ignored. Potentially there were others during his childhood experience on the plantation which, for someone with his particular background, the social order simply did not make available. But
Sutpen, as we have seen, comes totally to express the very inhumanity

and injustice which he would have us believe compelled the "design"
in the first place. When Judith's life is ruined as a consequence of the
complications which lead to the murder of Bon, she complains to
Quentin's grandmother that the fulfillment of her life was frustrated
by forces over which she had no control.

> Because you make so little impression, you see. You get born and you
> try this and don't know why only you keep on trying it and you are born
> at the same time with a lot of other people, all mixed up with them,
> like trying to, having to, move your arms and legs with strings only the
> same strings are hitched to all the other arms and legs and the others
> all trying and they don't know why either except that the strings are all
> in one another's way like five or six people all trying to make a rug on
> the same loom only each one wants to weave his own pattern into the
> rug . . . [p. 127].

Actually, it is her father's "innocence" of anything but his own compulsion which disorders her life and the lives of "a lot of other people."
Quentin, only with much pain, finally discovers in the career of Thomas
Sutpen not the essence of his past so much as a force which disrupts
all that was possibly coherent, orderly, and humane in the past.

Both in *Go Down, Moses* and in this novel, Faulkner clearly recog-
nizes the evil tendencies of the plantation system. But Sutpen acts as
a wholly "modern" element in that system. He unknowingly abstracts

those evil tendencies from the controlling fiber of the community and its traditions, simply exploiting them without discipline for the purposes of his own ambition. It is no wonder that Mr. Compson feels able to observe that perhaps the Civil War was "instigated by that family fatality" [p. 118] for which Sutpen is largely responsible. We are told that Rosa's father, who actually equates the force of the Civil War with the exploitations of his son-in-law, firmly believed that in both of these the South "was now paying the price for having erected its economic edifice not on the rock of stern morality but on the shifting sands of opportunism and moral brigandage" [p. 260]. Faulkner, in these and other remarks made in *Absalom, Absalom!,* gives full notice to the opinion that the true nature of the plantation system and of Sutpen's "design" was revealed negatively at the moment and in the act of breakdown.

But the novel itself does not allow us to be so categorical. We have already seen how factitious is so close an identification between the character of Sutpen and that of the social system he exploits. As Faulkner sees it, the system was corrupt enough not to be able to control its Thomas Sutpens. And we may even view the Civil War as a consequence of such a further corruption of existing order as that which was carried on by Sutpen. It is well to remember, however, that a civil war was lost by Jefferson, Mississippi, when Sutpen finished his home and married Ellen Coldfield in 1838. The terrible result of both his "design" and the war between the states was fratricide. Faulkner's metaphorical use of the Sutpen story does not go much further than that; it is never extended into allegory. Sutpen is not what is called the Old South, but rather a force in it which was so corrupting that possibly, as Quentin thinks Rosa believes, *"only through the blood of our men and the tears of our women could He stay this demon and efface his name and lineage from the earth"* [p. 11]. But such a statement, in itself, is merely a rephrasing of Quentin's problem and of the theme of the novel. Quentin is trying to find in the issues of the conflicts within the Sutpen family and within the community of Jefferson some expression of a sense of human and moral value.

The structure of *Absalom, Absalom!* is a reflection of both the nature and the method of Quentin's search, in a confusion of historical fact, for value. Consideration of that structure might begin simply by dividing the novel into two parts of four chapters each, leaving Rosa's monologue, which separates them by exclusively occupying all of Chapter V, for special consideration. The first four chapters, in which the whole of Sutpen's story is continually repeated with changing emphases, are really a dramatization of Quentin's activity at the sources of his information. In the last four chapters, during which he is at Harvard College, Quentin, with the help of his roommate, Shreve, pieces together all of the facts and opinions about the story held by

Rosa, his father, and his grandfather, along with a good deal of information which is apparently a part of his heritage. All of the data, as
it comes to him in the early chapters, is confused, contradictory,
and phenomenal in character. It is like the letter which Judith had
given to his grandmother and which is now a document in his attempt
to order the story coherently:

> the writing faded, almost indecipherable, yet meaningful, familiar in
> shape and sense, the name and presence of volatile and sentient forces;
> you bring them together in the proportions called for, but nothing
> happens; you re-read, tedious and intent, poring, making sure that you
> have forgotten nothing, made no miscalculation; you bring them together
> again and again nothing happens: just the words, the symbols, the shapes
> themselves, shadowy inscrutable and serene, against that turgid back-
> ground of a horrible and bloody mischancing of human affairs [p. 101].

The events of the Sutpen narrative are neither so contemporary
nor, except for Rosa, so personally consequential to the speakers here
as are those in *The Sound and the Fury*. Yet neither Rosa nor Mr.
Compson, both of whom first tell the story to Quentin in the early
chapters, are wholly trustworthy narrators. In the first chapter, Quentin becomes directly involved in the story, parts of which he has heard
throughout his childhood, when he visits Rosa Coldfield in compliance
with a note she has sent him. Before revealing the task she has planned,
Rosa, by way of justifying herself, begins to tell her version of Sutpen's
character and activity. As he listens, Quentin does not yet realize that,
like her handwriting, Rosa's "demonizing" of Sutpen is indicative of
a character which is "cold, implacable, and even ruthless" [p. 10].
Her description of Sutpen's first years in Jefferson is wild and incredible. Sutpen becomes *"an ogre, some beast out of tales to frighten
children with"* [p. 158]. But the distortions resulting from her night-
marish sensibility are continually being revealed to the reader by the
contradictory nature of Rosa's own testimony. At other times, her version of an incident may remain consistent throughout her conversation,
only to be invalidated by some other narrator who is either more
informed or at least less prejudiced. Her "outraged recapitulation"
evokes for Quentin a vision of Sutpen's arrival in Jefferson—"Out of
quiet thundercap he would abrupt (man-horse-demon) . . . with
grouped behind him his band of wild niggers like beasts" [p. 8]. We
are given quite a different picture, however, in the next chapter. Mr.
Compson describes Sutpen's first appearance in Jefferson as it was
viewed by Quentin's grandfather. We see in place of Rosa's "demon,"
a man "gaunt now almost to emaciation" [p. 32] trying to reach his
property before dark so that he can find food for his Negroes, who,
though wild, sit quietly in the wagon. The point is not that Rosa is
unfair to Sutpen. He is a "demon" to be sure. But, as I hope to show

presently, her reasons for calling him one are as ambiguous and questionable as her version of the event just discussed.

The detailing of incidents by Quentin's father, in Chapters II, III, and IV, if not as distorted as Rosa's, is no less riddled with faulty information. On the basis of what he knows, Mr. Compson believes, for example, that Sutpen forbade Judith's marriage merely because her fiancé, Charles Bon, kept an octoroon mistress in New Orleans. Considering the final consequences of the father's refusal, Mr. Compson understandably remarks: "It's just incredible. It just does not explain" [p. 100]. But Quentin, after his trip to Sutpen's Hundred with Rosa, comes into possession of more information. In the process of retelling the story in Chapter VII, he corrects his father's error in Chapter II. We learn what only Sutpen knew at the time: the real identity of Charles Bon. Judith's betrothal to him was forbidden by Sutpen because it would have resulted not only in incest, but in miscegenation. This new information not only partially invalidates Mr. Compson's analysis, but also reflects adversely on the already questionably account of the story given by Rosa. In the first chapter she tells Quentin that she "saw Judith's marriage forbidden without rhyme or reason or shadow of excuse" [p. 18]. It is this belief, based on ignorance of the facts, which partly explains the peculiar quality of her hatred of Sutpen. Rosa's bitterness and frustration at being the last child of cold and unloving parents finds total expression in the collapse of the romantic life she had lived vicariously in that of her niece, Judith.

In the light of the new facts uncovered by Quentin, the reader must now re-evaluate Rosa's emotional state which has its reference in the incredibility for her of Sutpen's prohibition of the marriage. By doing so the reader sees that the attitude of Rosa, or it might be of any other narrator, is understandable not in terms of what actually has happened but because of either her lack of information or her inability to change her mind when new information is made available. To Quentin's already prodigious task of finally ordering the story is added the responsibility of reinterpreting all that Rosa has told him and, at the same time, of giving an understandable context to her "incredulous and unbearable amazement" [p. 14]. Quentin's version of the Judith–Bon affair causes a reorientation of the whole Sutpen story. Sutpen's attitude toward the marriage becomes a coherent element in his "design" and Bon's insistence on returning to marry his half-sister becomes a dramatically powerful gesture activated by his need for paternal recognition.

This correction of Mr. Compson's statement in Chapter IV [p. 100] by Quentin in Chapter VII [p. 266] is superficially indicative of the form of the novel. But as I have pointed out, the dramatization in the early chapters of Quentin's attempt to assemble all the facts is separated from his painful effort in the later chapters meaningfully

to order this material by the long soliloquy of Rosa Coldfield. The
novel seems to turn upon her chapter. Indeed, before Quentin begins
to piece the whole story together in his room at Harvard, the opposition to Sutpen seems most strenuously represented by her.

Before dealing with Rosa Coldfield in greater detail, I want to
suggest once again that the emphasis here is primarily upon Quentin,
that neither Rosa nor Sutpen can serve as the dramatic center of this
novel. Quentin's acts of remembrance actually determine the form of
the novel. Rosa's soliloquy is apparently a product of her mind. But
it is presented as if it were being recalled in Quentin's even as he sits
listening to her. Before he and Shreve begin the job of historical recrea-
tion, Quentin can see in Rosa's approach to the Sutpen story the great
difficulty which will beset him in his effort to discover the human
content of his heritage. From her involvement in the "design," Rosa
seems to conclude that history fulfills itself not through the efforts or
aspirations of human beings, but wholly in an impersonal, antagonistic universe, through abstract "designs" or by the action of Fate. If
that is the case, Quentin's tradition is devoid of human value. Eventually, his attempt to discover a meaningful tradition depends for its
success upon his discovery of a participant in the conflict with Sutpen
with whom he can share an active sense of association. Whoever that
individual is, he must be able, as Rosa is not, to acknowledge the
world outside himself; he must surrender some of his individuality
in order actively to participate in society. Rosa simply compounds for
Quentin the already frightening phenomena of Sutpen. She is no more
aware than her "demon" of any necessary relationship between her
aspirations and the moral codes and social disciplines of the community.

Considering the possibility that Sutpen's "design" has denied to
Rosa any hope for the future, it is a not-unimportant irony, for its
effect on the total meaning of the novel, that Rosa's association with
Sutpen is actually only intermittent and largely vicarious. Even before
seeing him for the first time, Rosa is conditioned by her guardian, a
spinster aunt, to think of Sutpen as an "ogre," a "demon." Her only
direct involvement with him, other than the yearly visits discontinued
at her father's death, occurs when Miss Rosa is Judith's companion
and Sutpen suddenly proposes to her. But the most injurious contact
exists without Sutpen's knowledge and operates in Miss Rosa's dream
state as part of her romantic illusions about Charles Bon.

Although she has never seen him, Rosa has fallen deeply in love
with her vision of the man who she never learns is Sutpen's unrecog-
nized son. She has heard him discussed by Ellen, whose plans for an
engagement between him and Judith, also made in ignorance of Bon's
identity, come to objectify Rosa's own romantic longings. Her dream
of Bon is a dream of a future, a "living fairy tale" [p. 76]. Like Sut-

pen's dream of the future, it is a "fairy tale" which is foolishly isolated ' from the world of other human beings in which it must, if at all, exist. Rosa's dream was concocted in the hallways of her darkened house. Only there could she remain *"shod with the very damp and velvet silence of the womb"* [p. 145], unapprehended by what she calls *"some cold head-nuzzling forceps of the savage time"* [p. 144].

When Wash Jones shouts beneath her window that Henry has "kilt" Charles Bon "dead as a beef" [p. 133], she leaves this "hallway" and rushes out to Sutpen's Hundred. She does not go, as she claims, to rescue Judith from the curse which seems to be on the house. Rather, she is trying desperately to save some of the enchantment of Judith's proposed wedding, her own "vicarious bridal" [p. 77]. But when she rushes into the hall calling for Judith, her *"shadow-realm of make-believe"* [p. 147] comes into direct conflict with Sutpen's *"factual scheme"* [p. 143]. This is embodied for Rosa in Clytie, Sutpen's daughter by a Negro slave and, Rosa claims, *"his own image the cold Cerberus of his private hell"* [p. 136]. Clytie has blocked Rosa's path, which leads to Judith's room, to Bon's body, which has been placed there. The moment of conflict has finally been achieved. But even Rosa knows that her involvement in the Sutpen tragedy is indirect: *"we seemed to glare at one another not as two faces but as two abstract contradictions which we actually were"* [p. 138].

At this point the narrative stops. Attention is focused by Rosa upon the significance of Clytie's grip on her arm. She cries out, not at Clytie but at what she calls the *"cumulative over-reach of despair itself"* [p. 140]. In attempting to define its elements, Rosa expands this single moment, which is in a sense out of time, into her whole experience of life. Her immediate response becomes enlarged into the total response of an individual who has encountered the disabling grip of a damaging past as she tries to realize her dream of the future. But even as she stands there, Rosa persists in believing that there *"is a might-have-been which is more true than truth"* [p. 143]. Only when she is released by Clytie are her illusions completely shattered. She finds that though Bon is dead, she still is denied by Judith the chance to look at him, that Judith, left nearly a widow, refuses to grieve for him. Rosa at last faces what Sutpen optimistically refused to face: *"that sickness somewhere at the prime foundation of this factual scheme"* [p. 143]. That "sickness," one might say, is primarily an ignorance of context. The pattern of events which Rosa had chosen to recognize was only a dream. One action, which to a narrator like Quentin might fit naturally into the sequence of events, can suddenly thrust a *"maelstrom of unbearable reality"* [p. 150] into her dream life.

The collapse of Rosa's illusions is roughly equivalent to Sutpen's sudden discovery, also due to Bon's activity, that in pursuit of his "design" he seems to have arrived "at a result absolutely and forever incredible" [p. 263]. Sutpen still believes that it is merely a matter of miscalculation and that "whether it was a good or a bad design is beside the point" [p. 263]. But he feels compelled to go to General Compson in order to "review the facts for an impartial . . . mind to examine and find and point out to him" his mistake [p. 267]. Similarly, Rosa must reassess her whole experience in relation to her fatal excursion into the "factual scheme" of things. And she tells the story of her life to Quentin after she has experienced the effects of having been awakened out of the dream state. The shock and revulsion resulting from the stair episode is imposed back upon situations from which the necessity of Rosa's emotions would not seem naturally to have arisen. Rosa can acknowledge the past only through the retroactive distortions of her own rage and frustration. Her version of the story is infinitely more complex than Sutpen's. But it cannot assist Quentin in his task even as much as that superficial outline of his experience which is all Sutpen could give to General Compson.

The poverty of Sutpen's imagination and the neurotic richness of Rosa's place the two figures at poles. Yet in their different ways, both express a wholly nonsocial, dangerously individualistic point of view. This polar equality between Sutpen and Rosa is similar in kind to the thematic relationship existing in *Light in August* between Hightower and Joe Christmas, neither of whom even meet until the climax of that novel. Hightower's hysterical suggestion that he and Joe Christmas had spent the evening of the murder in an illicit relationship is only factually implausible. Rosa and Sutpen were, as pathetically, made for each other. That is the ironic appropriateness of Sutpen's proposal. What Rosa confesses to Quentin, and to us, is the story of a woman who, confronting a world as furiously antagonistic as Sutpen's, feels that she can come to life only as a man:

> But it was no summer of a virgin's itching discontent; no summer's caesarean lack which should have torn me, dead flesh or even embryo, from the living: or else, by friction's ravishing of the male-furrowed meat, also weaponed and panoplied as a man instead of hollow woman [p. 145].

It is sufficient to say that Sutpen represents all that she would but cannot be. In her soliloquy he is given alternately the face of an ogre and the *"shape of a hero"* [p. 167]. She recalls that her life *"was at last worth something"* [p. 162] when she helped care for him after the war. His proposal is accepted simply because he is a man and, she thinks then, a heroic one: she *"lost all the shibboleth erupting of cannot, will not, never will in one red instant's fierce obliteration"* [p. 163]. The breaking of the engagement occurs only when he intimates that she is merely the means to provide him with another son to carry on the "design." In a rage, she returns to her "womb-like corridor" [p. 112] to live on the charity of the town and to continue her "demonizing" of Sutpen, a role which her aunt "seems to have invested her with at birth along with the swaddling clothes" [p. 61].

But the very attitudes implicated in her final revulsion and hatred of Sutpen further the ironic similarities already suggested as existing between Sutpen and Rosa Coldfield. Both of them try desperately to disown the past. Rosa has had her own design, one by which she was obsessed with a future even more impossible of achievement than Sutpen's. Sutpen's scapegoat is the "monkey nigger"; Rosa's is Sutpen. She uses him, as Sutpen used his experience at the plantation door, to objectify an exclusively egocentric and romantic view of life which has been wrenched apart by forces and events for which she holds this remarkably childish man too exclusively responsible. She never sees in the very nature of her illusions—nor does he in his—the source of their destruction.

Faulkner's own literary position is powerfully suggested by the dramatic function in the novel of Rosa's self-negating soliloquy. Chapter V is comparable, in this respect, to Yeats's poem *Meditations in Time of Civil War*. If I read that poem correctly, it dramatizes the dilemma of a literary artist attempting to find his metaphors in an unsettled society, a society bent on disvaluation. Recognizing this feature in *Absalom, Absalom!*, one is almost obliged to associate the problems of the author with the problems of Quentin Compson. In Rosa Coldfield's soliloquy, Faulkner has dramatically fused literary with social disorders. These very disorders are in large part what T. S. Eliot is concerned with in *After Strange Gods*. Both Rosa's point of view and the career of Thomas Sutpen, which concerns her, are illustrative of the heretical sensibility on the loose, of the danger, which Eliot defines for us, of overindulgent individualism: "when morals cease to be a matter of tradition and orthodoxy . . . and when each man is to elaborate his own, then *personality* becomes a thing of alarming importance." [8]

This sort of "elaboration" is clearly dramatized by Rosa's obliviousness to anything but her own needs and compulsions. But its literary applications are made most evident by the stylistic quality of her version of the Sutpen story. Through the style of Rosa's soliloquy, we are made aware that Sutpen is not alone in his pursuit of "strange Gods." A rather peculiar Eros intrudes upon Agape despite Rosa's incantations to an avenging God. Perhaps because of this, her soliloquy is reminiscent of the Gerty McDowell sequence in Joyce's *Ulysses*. Such a parallel is particularly noticeable in those passages in which Rosa's poetic sensibility seems to function in the soul of a pathetic, antebellum "bobby-soxer." She remarks of Bon's picture:

[8] P. 54.

And I know this: if I were God I would invent out of this seething turmoil we call progress something (a machine perhaps) which would adorn the barren mirror altars of every plain girl who breathes with such as this—which is so little since we want so little—this pictured face. It would not even need a skull behind it; almost anonymous, it would only need vague inference of some walking flesh and blood desired by someone else even if only in some shadow-realm of make-believe [p. 147].

Such tortuous, verbalized relieving of emotion, and there are more obvious examples throughout this soliloquy, is a consequence of Rosa's neurotic self-absorption. She is bringing herself to life through emotional paroxysms. Eliot observes much the same thing happening, but not with Faulkner's ironic purpose, in the novels of Hardy. Indeed, Eliot's definition of the kind of "heresy" Hardy is supposed to have committed in his novels applies exactly to those qualities of Rosa's soliloquy which I am anxious to point out. Eliot observes

> . . . an interesting example of a powerful personality uncurbed . . . by submission to any objective beliefs; unhampered by any ideas, or even by what sometimes acts as a partial restraint . . . the desire to please a large public. [Hardy] . . . seems to me to have written as nearly for the sake of self-expression as a man well can. . . .[9]

The point I should like to make is that Eliot's remarks can apply to Rosa but cannot in any sense be applied to Faulkner. This is precisely the mistake made by those critics who have accused Faulkner of being irresponsibly romantic. Mr. Alfred Kazin, for example, asserts that Faulkner represents "a tormented individualism in the contemporary novel, a self-centered romanticism." [10] If this were true, we might use Rosa Coldfield's soliloquy to direct irony against the author himself. Obviously, the novel does not allow us to do this. The context in which Faulkner places her soliloquy prevents it from having any persuasively incantatory effect upon the reader. Rosa's romantic verbalization is consistent with her avocation as a poet but reflects only in a most negative way Faulkner's sense of his own vocation. When Quentin first visits Rosa, he remarks that even in his father's youth she had composed over one thousand poems to the soldiers of the Confederacy,

> . . . had already established herself as the town's and county's poetess laureate by issuing to the stern and meager subscription list of the county newspaper poems, ode, eulogy and epitaph, out of some bitter and implacable reserve of undefeat [p. 11].

[9] *Ibid.*
[10] Alfred Kazin, *On Native Grounds* (New York, 1942), p. 466. See also J. Donald Adams, *The Shape of Books to Come* (New York, 1944), p. 131; Elizabeth Hardwick, "Faulkner and the South Today," *Partisan Review*, October, 1948, pp. 1130–35; Granville Hicks, *The Great Tradition* (New York, 1935), p. 291; Wyndham Lewis, *Men Without Art* (London, 1934), pp. 44–48; Edmund Wilson, "William Faulkner's Reply to the Civil Rights Program," *The New Yorker*, October 23, 1948, p. 106.

The "undefeat" of what? Certainly not the war, since Rosa pretends on several occasions to subscribe to the moral necessity of the South's defeat. Rosa's indiscriminate outrage has a primarily personal and an ambiguously sexual content. Quentin, even before he begins his re-creation of the story, listens to Rosa as the last and most vociferous opponent of Sutpen. But the reader will be disappointed who tries to discover in Rosa's soliloquy the moral basis for her hatred of Sutpen. All that she can reveal to Quentin is the "undefeat" not of moral rigor but of an essentially unregenerate personality.

When Rosa is finished, Sutpen remains where Quentin found him, bewilderingly inexplicable. The explanation for this is part of the logic of Faulkner's method which is really the method of historical research and re-creation. But the historical method has to this point proved, so far as Quentin is concerned, tragically unsuccessful. Rosa's inability to place events in their human and historical context, an inability which she shares with Sutpen, results quite naturally in the treatment of both individuals and complex social action as phenomena. The "phenomenon" for Sutpen was the "monkey nigger." It compelled the "design." Rosa's inability to give human proportions to Sutpen, "the demon," results eventually in her romantic and pessimistic view of history. The implications are obvious. Both Rosa and Sutpen are really ignorant of what is going on about them. Knowledge is the basis of historical perspective and knowledge is essentially an act of remembrance, an awareness of tradition.[11]

The form of *The Sound and the Fury*, of *Absalom, Absalom!*, and of most of Faulkner's major works is determined by this conception. The reader is witness to a conscious stockpiling of information by the characters as the story is repeated over and over again with a different focus upon the material, a persistent encirclement of alien facts and enigmatic personalities by all the accumulated knowledge of an individual, a family, or an entire community. In *Knight's Gambit*, this form is used to allow a gathering of anecdotes by the attorney Gavin Stevens from the whole countryside. Eventually, the form of each of Gavin's stories is the same as the process of community justice in the solution of the crime and in the judging of the criminal.

Quentin's persistent acts of remembrance in the last four chapters finally are successful in placing Sutpen in a comprehensible human context. Quentin and his roommate, Shreve McCannon, bring both a fairly complete knowledge of the facts and an inventive curiosity to the job of historical re-creation. Sutpen himself ceases to be a phenomenon in Quentin's past.

In their final ordering of the story, Quentin and Shreve are primarily concerned with the activity of Charles Bon and Henry Sutpen.

[11] I am remembering some observations by Nicholas Berdyaev on the general problem of value in history. Nicholas Berdyaev, *The Meaning of History* (London, 1936).

Quentin's perceptive awareness of the meaning of that activity infuses a wholly human content into what has been the mechanical abstract nature of those past experiences which seem to constitute his heritage. It is specifically this human content, we have seen, which Sutpen tacitly ejected from his "design" by his refusal ever to recognize Bon as his son. And it is ironic, in view of Quentin's presentation of Bon, that in Rosa's soliloquy, as well as in Mr. Compson's version of the story, Sutpen is never more inhuman. Rosa herself never seems more fantastic than in [her version of] their relationships to Charles Bon.

The account of the Bon story which finally emerges from the conversations of Quentin and Shreve may be viewed as an attempted rejection by Quentin of both his father's and Rosa's points of view. The effect, in terms of the novel, is a rejection of naturalism. The activity of Bon and Henry, as it is seen by Quentin, simply does not sustain a conception of history either as an impersonal mechanism or in which "blind Fate" slowly and solemnly triumphs. Faulkner quite admirably makes his own job extremely difficult. He endows Bon's career with all the material which should by its very nature keep Rosa's "current of retribution and fatality" [p. 269] moving on unaffected by Bon's own feelings and desires. Bon's childhood, according to Shreve, was almost a ritual in which his mother prepared him as an agent of her revenge on her husband. And, as we have already seen, Bon's experience at Sutpen's Hundred is made equivalent to that of Sutpen as a child standing before the plantation door.

Actually, however, Bon gives Sutpen numerous opportunities to correct his "mistake." Rather than revenge for his mother, all he is seeking is his father *"out of the shadow of whose absence my spirit's posthumeity has never escaped"* [p. 317]. If Sutpen had for one moment equally transcended the effects of his childhood and of his repudiation, if he had once perceived Bon's human motive, then the latter would, he claims, have sacrificed the love of Henry and whatever claim he might have to the love of Judith:

> *Yes. Yes. I will renounce her; I will renounce love and all; that will be cheap, cheap, even though he say to me "never look upon my face again; take my love and my acknowledgment in secret, and go" I will do that; I will not even demand to know of him what it was my mother did that justified his action toward her and me* [p. 327].

But he at last falls victim, as Sutpen himself is a victim, to the ravages of this abstract "design." Incest with Judith or death at the hands of his brother become the only ways in which Bon can identify himself as Sutpen's son. Henry, after four years of painful indecision, kills his friend and brother at the gates of Sutpen's Hundred. For Bon, this was the ultimate recognition of his sonship. For Henry, it was a terribly difficult moral act. It had to be carried out in a world which his father, like Quentin's mother in *The Sound and the Fury,* has almost wholly corrupted. Henry acts not in obedience to his father, but to an inherent sense of a moral code which is stronger than his love for Bon. The act, though Sutpen insisted upon it, is really a transcendence by Henry of the dehumanized quality of his father's "design." This part of the story is proof for Quentin, if he needed proof, that life in the past was not as easily heroic as his father once imagined, the circumstances neither so "simple" nor the people so "distinct, uncomplex." What is important is that Quentin can see in the activity of Charles and Henry an active expression, however confused and frustrated, of human value responding to the inhumanity of Sutpen.

Shreve is genuinely moved by the account he and Quentin are able to make of Bon's and Henry's dilemmas. By the time that element of the story is finished, he has ceased both his self-conscious demonizing of Rosa and the picayune, witty interjections at which Quentin is silently but visibly annoyed. At one point, both he and Quentin become so engrossed in their own efforts fully to re-create the story that "it did not matter to either of them which one did the talking" [p. 316]. As the story develops, it becomes profoundly human, profoundly noumenal in content. So much so that for the first time the two boys at Harvard find themselves understandably situated within the destinies of the "shades" they create:

> They were both in Carolina and the time was forty-six years ago, and it was not even four now but compounded still further since now both of them were Henry Sutpen and both of them were Bon [p. 351].

But the conversations of Quentin and Shreve do not end with the killing of Bon, with a personal action carried out in painful recognition of a moral code. As they continue with the Sutpen story, its natural sequence is significantly disrupted. Chronologically, though all of the details are made available to us in earlier chapters, the death of Bon should be followed by Wash Jones's murder of Thomas Sutpen and by the violent escapades of Bon's son, Valery Bon, who has been brought by Clytie and Judith to Sutpen's Hundred. Structurally, however, the next incident with which Quentin and Shreve concern themselves is the final catastrophe of the Sutpen family, a catastrophe which seems to affirm the workings of a grotesquely deterministic universe. Such a focus on the material as a chronological ordering of the Wash Jones and Valery Bon stories would have allowed might have permitted Quentin a more substantial mitigation of the meaning which Shreve desperately assigns in the end to the idiot who alone survives at Sutpen's Hundred.

The actions of Wash Jones and of Valery Bon suggest as clearly as the final actions of Bon and Henry a distorted but eloquent sense of moral revulsion at the corruption and inhumanity of Sutpen's "design." When there seems no hope of reinstituting that "design," Sutpen perhaps consciously provokes Wash into killing him. In Wash's hearing, he crudely repudiates Milly, Wash's granddaughter, when she fails to bear him a son. But we can as easily view the murder less as a credit to Sutpen's scheming than as an assertion by Wash of human pride. In order to reaffirm his manhood and his dignity, he must destroy the man who has been his hero. His conduct partakes of the same traditional morality which justifies, in the short story "Tomorrow," the murder of Buck Thorpe by an outraged father. The murder in both instances can be viewed as punishment for a gross violation of primitive social mores.

Like Milly and Wash, Valery Bon discovers that he, too, is a part of the rejected residue of his grandfather's career. His subsequent conduct is a comment upon the consequences of Sutpen's invalidation of the habits and customs of the community which, taken together, constitute a kind of moral or social discipline. Having no family of his own, his real identity hidden from the town, Valery Bon seeks literally to make a name for himself by violent and extraordinary action. Though he could pass for a white man, he marries a woman who is an extremely dark Negress, and insists on being recognized as a Negro himself. Considering the social consequences, this is really a conscious form of self-degradation similar in its motivation to that of Joe Christmas in *Light in August*. Valery Bon's violence, like Joe's unkindness to Mrs. McEachern, is directed against the feminizing pity of those about him. They are aware of their own incompleteness; and symbolically this may be viewed as a dimly Christian awareness of the possible glory of being human. Joe and Valery Bon can define themselves only horribly. In Sutpen's world, all Valery Bon can do is to assert negatively his potential dignity as a man.

But the structure of the final episodes dramatically excludes from the immediate attention of Quentin and Shreve the moral affirmations, however deformed, of Wash and Valery Bon. Instead, we have in the sharpest possible juxtaposition, the circumstances of Bon's death and the almost theatrical horror of the burning of Sutpen's Hundred. Valery Bon's son, the heir to the estate and a Negro idiot, is left to "lurk around those ashes and howl" [p. 376]. The howling of Jim Bond is totally devoid of the kind of value which was tragically dramatized by Henry's murder of his friend. Quentin actually trembles in his bed as he remembers it.

The structure insists on the persistent quality of Quentin's problem. The Negro idiot seems powerfully to reintroduce the apparently inhuman and mechanistic nature of Sutpen's history and of Quentin's heritage. Shreve is moved almost as much as Quentin by the ambiguous quality of the story they have finally pieced together, by the insoluble tension between the human needs and passions inherent in the tale and the impersonally deterministic form it seems to take. But he rather pathetically disguises his feelings and doubts. He grasps what is for him the easiest solution, what is for Quentin an emotionally impossible solution—the cliché of the idiot as symbol of predestined doom. This final catastrophe, he tells Quentin, "clears the whole ledger, you can tear all the pages out and burn them, except for one thing" [p. 378]. That one thing, Shreve facetiously concludes, is the mechanism itself by which "the Jim Bonds are going to conquer the western hemisphere":

> So it took Charles Bon and his mother to get rid of old Tom, and Charles Bon and the octoroon to get rid of Judith, and Charles Bon and Clytie to get rid of Henry; and Charles Bon's mother and Charles Bon's grandmother got rid of Charles Bon. So it takes two niggers to get rid of one Sutpen, dont it? [pp. 377–378].

Shreve ends his remarks, to which Quentin has listened silently and unwillingly, with a final question: "Why do you hate the South?" What he assumes is that Quentin can afford to hate not simply the South, but his past, his paternity, and himself as a product of all three.

Quentin gives the only possible answer with a terrifying urgency:

> "I dont hate it," Quentin said, quickly, at once, immediately; "I dont hate it," he said. *I dont hate it* he thought, panting in the cold air, the iron New England dark; *I dont. I dont! I dont hate it! I dont hate it!*

His only other possible answer would be a telling of the whole story of Sutpen over again. But Quentin speaks to himself as much as to his friend. Annoying to Quentin as Shreve's easy and terrible solution might seem, the possibility exists for him even at the end of the novel that man and his history are mutually hostile and alien; that he is merely the reflex of some impersonal and abstract historical process. But it is a possibility to which he refuses wholly to succumb. Inherent in the tragically suggestive ambiguity of the conclusion is the justification for the structure of *Absalom, Absalom!* The form of the novel itself insists that the act of placing Sutpen in the understandable context of human society and history is a continually necessary act, a never-ending responsibility and an act of humanistic faith.

Hardy, Faulkner, and the
Prosaics of Tragedy

by John Paterson

. . . *The Mayor of Casterbridge* reinstates, to begin with, the Aristotelian relation between plot and character which the novel has
tended to reverse. Traditional rather than improvised, fabulous in the
sense that the plots of *Oedipus* and *Lear* are fabulous, Hardy's plot
reaches to and exploits the primitive rhythms of a fundamental process, the immemorial contest between the old god, the old dispensation,
and the new. It possesses to this extent a life, an expressive value,
entirely its own. It does not merely exist, as in Dickens, to set character
in motion nor, as in George Eliot, to externalize the will of character
acting with or against the bias of environment. It enacts a universal
motion or movement greater than and exterior to both the will of
character and the bias of environment. Surrounded as he is by a pallid
aggregation of characters, the masterful figure of Michael Henchard
does dominate—as indeed he should—the world of the novel. But he
dominates it to the same extent—no less and no more—that Lear and
Oedipus dominate their worlds. Like them, he may contribute as
character to the action; but he is not, as character, its ultimate source.

If the fascinations of individual character are not indulged at the
expense of the plot, it is because the protagonist is not subjected to
the remorseless psychological analysis peculiar to novelistic form.
Rich, powerful, and various as it is, Henchard's inner life is rendered
almost entirely in terms of action and dialogue and, failing that, in
terms of a descriptive technique less reportorial than dramatic. His
reaction to his wife's sudden reappearance after twenty years is registered, for example, in a simple and unelaborated detail that renders
superfluous the minute analysis and exposition to which the novel's
interest in character generally leads it: "he sat in his dining-room
stiffly erect, gazing at the opposite wall as if he read his history
there." As a result, the personality of the protagonist remains to the
very end, as it does in the *Agamemnon* and *Oedipus Rex*, something

"*Hardy, Faulkner, and the Prosaics of Tragedy*" by John Paterson. *Excerpted from*
Centennial Review 5 (*1961*): *160–63, 166–75. Reprinted by permission of the author
and the publisher.*

of a miracle and a mystery. More important, the novel is spared, by its freedom from the psychological norm, that disproportionate emphasis on character that might have complicated at least its status as tragedy.

The Mayor of Casterbridge also restores the traditional relationship between scene or setting on the one hand and plot and character on the other. It expressly contravenes the novel's strong predisposition to exhibit character in terms of its "conditions." For Casterbridge does not surround and ultimately overwhelm the principals of the novel, has little of the density and depth of an Egdon Heath or a Middlemarch. Asserting itself scarcely more aggressively than the abstract settings of the Periclean and Elizabethan stages, the city remains discreetly in the background of the novel. Clym Yeobright seems so small because Egdon Heath looms so large behind him; Michael Henchard looms so large because Casterbridge seems so small. The technique responsible for the making of the protagonist is also responsible, in fact, for the making of the scene. Just as Henchard is not, like Dorothea Brooke or Eustacia Vye, required to sit for his portrait, Casterbridge is not, like Middlemarch or Egdon Heath, subjected to an elaborate and exhaustive set description. Entering the novel in pieces and fragments, it merges into and, like Henchard himself, is easily absorbed by, the principal effect of the plot. The emphasis on the natural or social surroundings that might have made for a gigantism of setting is equally repudiated with the psychological emphasis that might have made for a gigantism of character.

This is not to say that realistic elements do not enter the novel at all. While it does reenact a primitive universal process, it plainly exploits, in registering the impact of the new national culture on the ancient provincial culture of Wessex, the data of its particular time and place. *The Mayor of Casterbridge* is not compromised as tragedy, however, as *Tess* and *Jude* were to be compromised, and as it is in general the doom of the novel to be compromised, by a preoccupation with purely contemporary issues and conditions: *e.g.,* the predicament of the unwed mother in modern society and the validity (or invalidity) of the laws governing marriage. The conflict between the obsolescent agriculture that dates back to the Heptarchy and the new mechanized agriculture that comes in with the nineteenth century is not developed for its own sake but only insofar as it defines the tragic conflict between Henchard and Farfrae, the old dispensation and the new. The unspectacular materials of contemporary reality are assimilated by the tragic structure of the novel.

The Mayor of Casterbridge thus modifies, on behalf of its tragic motive, the novel's characteristic amplitude and elasticity of form, its democratic willingness to admit, as tragedy cannot safely do, the unblessed life of time and history. This is so much the case that Casterbridge's historical associations are more Roman and Hebraic than English. Michael Henchard is not after all the mayor of Dorchester, the provincial town whose reality is continuous with London and Liverpool and Manchester, but the mayor of Casterbridge, the provincial capital whose reality is continuous with Thebes, Padan-Aram, and ancient Rome. If his status and stature as tragic hero are not compromised by his membership in the antiheroic middle class, if he is more the tribal chieftain than the modern mayor, it is because Casterbridge suggests, with its agrarian economy, with its merchant aristocracy and its rude population of mechanics, artisans, and laborers, a primitive hierarchic society biblical or Roman in its simplicity. *The Mayor of Casterbridge* illustrates that the novel can fulfill its primary obligation to be lifelike, to represent the specific conditions of a time and place, and at the same time so far transcend them, so far reduce them to means, as to satisfy the more artistic, more artificial, requirements of tragedy.

The preeminence of plot and character as the chief agents of the tragic effect is guaranteed, finally, both by Hardy's adaptation of the omniscient convention and by the unspectacular simplicity of his prose. Using the referential language traditional with prose fiction, Aristotelian Hardy subordinates the arts of language to the primary impression of plot and character. Of all his novels, furthermore, *The Mayor of Casterbridge* suffers least from the interventions of a didactic and moralizing author. Though the voice of the novel is the voice of the author, it comes not from the foreground but, faintly and only intermittently, from the background. Taking much of the force out of Aristotle's dictum that tragedy must assume the form of action rather than of narrative, Hardy's epic author does not destroy that intense illusion of reality which the tragic novelist must maintain if he is to compete on equal terms with the dramatist. *The Mayor of Casterbridge* suggests, in short, that the novel may adapt itself to even the most stringent necessities of tragic form without doing violence to the necessities of its own.[1] . . .

As prejudicial to the cause of tragedy as the cult of the symbol has been the cult of style in modern fiction. The peculiarity of every major innovation in the art of fiction over the last hundred years—of the Jamesian point of view and the Joycean stream of consciousness as well as of the symbolist method—is that it has called for a general heightening and intensification of the prose idiom. Language has been required to approximate the condition of lyric poetry, to carry a weight that the antediluvian novel, with its more objective orienta-

---

[1] In "*The Mayor of Casterbridge* as Tragedy," *Victorian Studies* (December, 1959), I tried to show that the tragic values and assumptions animating the novel were as traditional, as archaistic, as its form and technique.

tion, did not find necessary. As a result of this development, prose fiction has acquired in our time a new aesthetic respectability and prestige. But if Aristotle was right in claiming that the tragic effect was less a function of language and style than a function of character and plot, and there is little in the literature of tragedy to prove him wrong, then the modern novel's rhetorical complexity and richness would seem, from the point of view of tragedy, more a bane than a blessing. Joining with the dramatic point of view, the stream of consciousness method, and the art of the symbolist to attenuate or obscure the primary images of character and action, the rhetorical emphasis prevents the novel from exploiting the very sources that have made in the past for the great vitality of tragedy. Faulkner's *Absalom, Absalom!* is a case in point. Eventually more formidable as a work of art and certainly more complete as a novel than Hardy's *The Mayor of Casterbridge, Absalom, Absalom!* seems, when the two are put together, conspicuously inferior as tragedy.

Defined more than once as an authentic and fully developed tragedy,[2] Faulkner's novel shows remarkably fundamental identities with Hardy's tragic masterpiece. As a fable of the glory and grotesqueness of man's destiny on earth, Thomas Sutpen's rise and fall is not, after all, very different from Michael Henchard's. If Hardy's hero has been driven by his hunger for worldly power and his impatience with domestic restraints to sell his wife to a sailor for five guineas, Faulkner's has been driven, by the same hunger and impatience, to commit the same crime: to repudiate the Haitian wife whose Negro blood stood in the way of his ambition. If Henchard's Faustian violation of his solidarity with man and nature has given him the illegitimate power and freedom to become the chief political and financial force in the community, Sutpen's has given him the same freedom and power and enabled him to realize the same basic design: to build a plantation, marry a respectable woman, and reign in baronial splendor over a large domain. The overweening pride, the psychological necessity, responsible for the original crime condemns Sutpen, like Henchard, finally, to commit the same crime over and over again and, again like Henchard, to create the conditions of his own disaster.

There are, of course, significant differences in emphasis. Though both Hardy and Faulkner can evoke the reality of a moral force in the universe against which man can offend and by which he can be punished, Faulkner's assumptions are naturalistic to a degree that

[2] See Cleanth Brooks, "*Absalom, Absalom!* The Definition of Innocence," *Sewanee Review*, LIX (Autumn, 1951), 543–558; Walter L. Sullivan, "The Tragic Design of *Absalom, Absalom!*," *South Atlantic Quarterly*, L (October, 1951), 552–566; Ilse Dusoir Lind, "The Design and Meaning of *Absalom, Absalom!*," *PMLA*, LXX (December, 1955), 887–912. See also Richard Sewall's discussion of *Absalom, Absalom!* in *The Vision of Tragedy*.

Hardy's are not. For Sutpen's arrogant and cruel aspiration a causal
explanation is, after all, produced in his humiliation as a boy at the
front door of a plantation owner: the "conditions" responsible for his
character, his monomania, are eventually accounted for. But no such
causal explanation, no such account, is offered for the moral defection
of Michael Henchard. Given no boyhood, no past that antedates his
startling crime in the first chapters of the novel, Henchard comes, as
it were, out of nowhere, the mysterious flaw in his character emerging
from and explained by no ascertainable "conditions." Moreover, since
the motive and the fate of Sutpen's private design is partially bound
up with the motive and the fate of the larger design of the South, he
becomes in part the victim of historical necessity. The necessity that
encompasses the fall of Michael Henchard, on the other hand, ema-
nates from a source outside rather than inside history. His defeat may
be associated with, but is not caused by, the disappearance of the old
agriculture and the accession of the new.

Hardy's novel closes, accordingly, on a note of grace altogether
missing in Faulkner's. In the absence of a mechanistic necessity, historical or otherwise, Henchard's disastrous end is prompted as much
by his own sense of guilt as by his pride. It is the condition of Sutpen's
downfall, on the other hand, that he can feel no sense of his own moral
dereliction, that he is capable neither of guilt nor of growth. Henchard
can thus be justified at last by his perception of the enormity of his
crime and the appropriateness of his punishment. But Sutpen is arrogant and blind to the very end. Henchard's death can suggest an act
of piety, an earnest of salvation, not very different from Lear's or An-
tony's; but Sutpen's is inevitably a slaughter, an earnest of damnation.
Henchard does not die to leave the world in darkness and ashes: sup-
planted in the persons of Farfrae and Elizabeth by simple imaginations untroubled by impious and grandiose ambitions, the old violent
sin-stained dispensation for which he stands gives way to a milder and
more humane order of things. With the grisly death of Thomas Sutpen, however, the light goes out as if forever. Succeeded not by the
Farfraes and Elizabeths, those pledges of a peaceful and pious future,
but by a totally demoralized Quentin Compson, Sutpen passes on not
a new and better world born out of the violence and ashes of the old,
but a ruined universe incapable of regeneration.

If *The Mayor of Casterbridge* is more successful as tragedy than
Absalom, Absalom!, however, it is not primarily for the reason that
Hardy's assumptions are less mechanistic than Faulkner's. It is primarily for the reason that Hardy, the provincial and the primitivist
as novelist, was profoundly indifferent to that revolution in form of
which Faulkner was to be the heir and beneficiary. It is for the reason,
in short, that Hardy's traditional and even rudimentary equipment as
a worker in the novel is ultimately more consistent with the purposes

of tragedy than Faulkner's elaborate poetics. Thus while the omniscient point of view in *The Mayor of Casterbridge* has the effect of insuring the continuity of the action, it is one of the necessary concomitants of the serial point of view employed by Faulkner that it makes for a fragmentation of the action. Registering itself as the possession of a removed and Olympian consciousness, the story of Michael Henchard advances in chronological time and hence can evoke a powerful sense of the inevitability of the hero's doom. Registered in the minds of four impassioned and even distracted narrators (Rosa Coldfield, Mr. Compson, Shreve McCannon, and Quentin Compson), the story of Thomas Sutpen exists only in psychological time and must sacrifice to this extent that sense of an inexorable march of events upon which the impact of tragedy at least partially depends.

Faulkner's serial point of view does have the effect of establishing distance between the reader and the principals of the action, an effect presumably justified by the authority of Greek tragedy. Placed as they are in the myth-making imaginations of Rosa Coldfield and Mr. Compson, the novel's chief agents are generalized as characters; freed from the restraints of a realistic psychology, they come to suggest the abstract creatures of classical tragedy. Henry Sutpen and Charles Bon can thus be described as existing "only to perform the parts assigned to them" and Clytie as serving "primarily to illuminate—not her own psychology—but the psychological, social, and moral aspects of the Negro–white conflict." [3] The problem of distance, however, is a problem more peculiar to the drama than to the novel; since the novelistic experience is less immediate than the dramatic experience, the problem of the novelist as tragic artist is less to create distance between the reader and his images than to remove it. The generalized character makes, moreover, a poor and unconvincing showing in a form that thrives on particularity. It offends against the sense of lifelikeness which is among the novelist's chief resources at the same time that it weakens the reader's identification with the protagonist which is among the tragedian's chief resources. If the point of Faulkner's narrative device was to establish distance between the reader and the principals of the action, the distaance turns out to have been too great.

It is the effect of Hardy's omniscient post of observation, above all, that it guarantees, in keeping with the Aristotelian dictum, the primary reality of character and plot. It is the effect of Faulkner's limited post (or posts) of observation, on the other hand, that it makes for a reduction of their reality. Told from the omniscient point of view, the action embodied in the story of Michael Henchard is located in the very foreground of the novel, its reality unconditioned and therefore undiminished by the intermediation of the interested nar-

[3] Lind, "The Design and Meaning of *Absalom, Absalom!*," pp. 888–9.

rator or narrators. Told from the point of view of four participants or observers all placed at various removes from the central action but all taking up positions within the framework of that action, the story of Thomas Sutpen, the basis of the novel's claims to tragic status, must necessarily retreat into the background, its reality as an action giving way to and obscured by the reality of the narrators as characters. The post of observation placed within the narrative framework does make, as James never tired of insisting, for vividness and concreteness of drama. The vital question for tragedy, however, is whether it is the subject or the object that has the benefit of the vividness and concreteness, and in the case of *Absalom, Absalom!*, the vividness and concreteness are more for the subject, for Rosa Coldfield and Quentin Compson, than for the object, for Thomas Sutpen and his tragic history. What occupies the novel, after all, is not the external drama of the hero but the internal drama of the narrators, their misrepresentations and distortions of the external drama, their investigation and final discovery of its central meaning. "It is Quentin's tragedy, above all, which the Sutpen tragedy must finally illuminate," one critic has recently explained.[4] But if it is Quentin's tragedy and not Sutpen's, then it is for obvious reasons no tragedy at all.

What makes all the difference, then, between *The Mayor of Casterbridge* and *Absalom, Absalom!*, what makes the one a tragedy and the other, albeit a bird of wondrous plumage, still a bird of quite another feather, is that where the plot in Hardy's novel has a life and a value of its own not variable with every unit of human consciousness, where it has in this degree a continuity in ontological or universal time, that same plot in Faulkner's novel achieves a continuity only in psychological time, alters in meaning from witness to witness, and is only stabilized, finally, as to its reality, in the problematical and hysterical consciousness of Quentin Compson. The plot, whose objectivity and whose independence of the vagaries of individual temperament were underwritten in *The Mayor of Casterbridge* by the illusion of an omniscient or absolute consciousness, declines in *Absalom, Absalom!* to a vibration in the agonized and finite consciousness of merely human observers, and is to this extent deprived of its power as the life and first principle of tragedy. The fate of character is to lose its reality in the same misty and mystic vibrations. For all the advantages in the way of vividness and concreteness that have been claimed for the dramatic point of view, Michael Henchard has a substantial reality which Sutpen, as the figment of a series of neurotic imaginations, cannot quite match. And having that reality, the illusion at least of objective reality, he can qualify as a tragic hero in a way that Sutpen cannot. Although it has currently been the fashion

[4] Lind, *op. cit.,* p. 893.

to denounce the omniscient convention as clumsy and old-fashioned, it is Hardy's stubborn orthodoxy in this connection that makes possible the specifically tragic consummation of *The Mayor of Casterbridge* at the same time that it is Faulkner's sophistication that militates against a specifically tragic consummation in *Absalom, Absalom!*

As damaging for the tragic purposes of Faulkner's novel is the rhetorical emphasis, the exploitation of purely stylistic resources, which is the usual concomitant of the dramatic point of view. In *The Mayor of Casterbridge,* the tragic intensity is a function not of rhetoric and style, but of the imagined material itself. Its language suggests not a crazy mirror in which character and incident are returned mutilated and distorted, but a clear window through which they are defined in lights and lines of their own. It acts with the omniscient point of view to produce that illusion of objectivity essential to the novel's status as a tragic experience. Required, on the other hand, to dramatize the passionate implication of the narrators, Faulkner's prose is so charged with the figures and rhythms of the language of poetry that it threatens to overwhelm the primary images of character and event. The tragic intensity that informs the novel becomes to a dangerous extent a product of the language rather than of the imagined material. The effects of character and plot are so far submerged in rhetorical effects, the vividness of the action is so far subordinated to the vividness of the emotions with which the narrators respond, that the novel's impact is eventually more melodramatic than dramatic, the restraint of tragic art giving way to the excess of gothic romance.

Already blurred and diffused by the complicated effects of language and point of view, the primary images of character and event are further diffused and blurred in *Absalom, Absalom!* by being called upon to assume a reality not intrinsically their own. Emblematic of Southern history, referring to something more or less or other than itself, the history of Thomas Sutpen loses the immediacy necessary to its impact and value as an authentically tragic action. To conceive the novel exclusively in terms of historical allegory is not, of course, to do it complete justice. "The undoing of Sutpen's false ambition," according to a recent critic, "illustrates the operation of retributive justice in the human drama; the fall of the South is its larger social representation." [5] But if Malcolm Cowley's contention that "with a little cleverness, the whole novel might be explained as a connected and logical allegory" [6] is wrong, it is not wrong enough. The correspondences between Sutpen's history and the history of the South may not dominate the novel, but they certainly condition it. The building of Sutpen's Hundred, the hero's alliance with the Calvinist shopkeeper

[5] Sullivan, "The Tragic Design of *Absalom, Absalom!*," p. 555.
[6] Malcolm Cowley, "Introduction," *The Viking Portable Faulkner* (New York, 1951), p. 13.

from the North, his repudiation and death at the hands of Wash
Jones: these derive much of their powerful reality as incidents from
their being conceived by the author and perceived by the reader within
the historical frame of reference.

The characters and events of the novel appear, for that matter,
within so many frames of reference operating simultaneously that
they can scarcely be visualized as having any reality outside them.
The religious and sexual idiosyncrasies of Rosa Coldfield's account
serve as a frame to give Sutpen a symbolic value as a demon, an ogre,
a species of Miltonic archangel, while Mr. Compson's temperamental
idiosyncrasies—his fatalism, his passion as gentleman and scholar for
the literature of Greek antiquity—act in the same fashion to give Sutpen his symbolic value as a hero in the tradition of classical tragedy.
The example of Greek tragedy exercises, in fact, an influence as a
frame of reference quite independently of Mr. Compson's intermittent
narrative contributions. "The continuing (though loose) analogies
which exist between Sutpen and Oedipus, Sutpen's sons and Eteocles
and Polyneices, Judith and Antigone, suggest," it has been said on
good authority, "that the Oedipus trilogy might have served as a general guide in the drafting of the plot." [7] Although an equally strong
case might be made for the *Oresteia* as a source, it should be clear
from this how little the characters and events of *Absalom, Absalom!,*
tangled as they are in a positive jungle of frames and symbols, can
emerge in lights and lines of their own and hence how little the Sutpen
story can materialize, for all its great intrinsic possibilities, as a fully
articulated tragedy.

The plot of *The Mayor of Casterbridge* itself is not, true enough,
sui generis. Michael Henchard's story bears striking resemblances to
the classical Oedipus legend and to the biblical Saul legend.[8] It is
bound up, too, like Sutpen's story, with the history of a particular time
and place, the conflict between the mayor and his antagonist referring
to the larger conflict between traditional and mechanical methods of
tilling the soil. Neither the literary nor the historic frames of reference, however—and they are hardly explicit enough to deserve the
name—so dominate the novel that character and action are translated
into that ulterior reality where images become symbols. The parallels
with Greek tragedy and Southern history are part of the very substance
of *Absalom, Absalom!,* but the parallels with Oedipus and Saul and
the history of local agriculture are no part of the substance of *The
Mayor of Casterbridge.* Hence the impact of Faulkner's novel depends,

---

[7] Lind, op. cit., pp. 889–890.

[8] See D. A. Dike, "A Modern Oedipus: *The Mayor of Casterbridge,*" *Essays in
Criticism,* II (April, 1952), 169–179; and Julian Moynahan, "*The Mayor of Caster-
bridge* and the Old Testament's First Book of Samuel: A Study of Some Literary
Relationships," *PMLA,* LXXI (March, 1956), 118–130.

as that of Hardy's does not, on our recognition of the analogies, on our intimations of the symbolic value of the characters and incidents. Sutpen must stand for the old economic dispensation of the South as Henchard is not required to stand for the old economic dispensation of Wessex.

Where Faulkner's hero has little value or reality, then, outside the symbolic dimensions established in the novel, Hardy's can claim reality and value as an image without ever having to claim reality and value as a symbol. And where the plot of Faulkner's novel is transvaluated by the literary and historical frames of reference, the plot of Hardy's novel does not require a greater valuation than it already possesses as a thing in itself. Henchard can be so very powerfully himself because he is not asked, like Sutpen, to be something or somebody else; and the action in which he participates can evoke so powerful a reality because, unlike that of *Absalom, Absalom!,* it is under no obligation to evoke a reality other than its own. The vitality of character and plot in *The Mayor of Casterbridge* is weakened no more by the vitality of the symbol than by the vitality of the narrator and the vitality of language. It is Hardy's freedom from Jamesian and Joycean sophistications in the art of the novel that makes possible the tragic consummation of *The Mayor of Casterbridge,* as it is Faulkner's commitment to these sophistications that prevents a tragic consummation in *Absalom, Absalom!*

A novel's qualifications as tragedy, or its lack of them, perhaps provide only very dubious grounds for critical discriminations. Less capable of envisioning the ultimate peace of traditional tragedy than Hardy was, more faithful to the terms of experience than to the arbitrary canons of a tragic art, Faulkner was evidently more concerned to define the tensions than to resolve them. If *Absalom, Absalom!* is disabled, then, as tragedy, it is only fair to suggest that it may have been prepared for other destinies, destinies different from but not necessarily inferior to those for which *The Mayor of Casterbridge* was evidently prepared. When all this has been said, however, there remains the hard consideration that if the novel cannot meet the challenge of tragedy, cannot rise to the most heroic perception of which the human imagination is capable, then a serious judgment on the limitations of its form, or on the limitations of the age that fathered the form, is necessarily involved. And if this is the case, then *The Mayor of Casterbridge* represents a more remarkable achievement than has generally been recognized. It demonstrates not only that the purposes of tragedy are better served by the old theory of the novel than by the new, but also that the historic recalcitrance of the form to the profundities of tragedy is by no means absolute. It demonstrates that there may be a prosaics as well as a poetics of tragedy.

Absalom, Absalom!

by Michael Millgate

The galleys of *Pylon* carry dates from early January 1935; the manuscript of *Absalom, Absalom!* is dated "March 30, 1935" on the first page and "31 January 1936" on the last.[1] On returning to *Absalom, Absalom!* after the period of respite or detour which had produced *Pylon* Faulkner must have begun his task virtually afresh, and in 1957 he said, "I don't remember at what point I put it [*Absalom, Absalom!*] down. Though when I took it up again I almost rewrote the whole thing. I think that what I put down were inchoate fragments that wouldn't coalesce and then when I took it up again, as I remember, I rewrote it."[2]

Some information as to the actual process of Faulkner's composition of *Absalom, Absalom!*, the steps by which he arrived at the intricate structure of the published book, may one day be gained from a closer study of the complete manuscript, which is now at the University of Texas. The first page of this manuscript is close to the published text,[3] but the manuscript as a whole is a composite, made up of material written at different times over what may have been a fairly long period. Many sections, some brief, some of one or more paragraphs in length, have been affixed to the base sheets, and these sections, like the base sheets themselves, are in a variety of different inks and even show minor differences in handwriting. It seems possible that careful study might reveal the outline of previous states of the manuscript material and thus throw valuable light on the construction of this most carefully articulated of Faulkner's novels.

Material representing other prepublication stages of *Absalom, Absalom!* is now at the University of Virginia. The typescript setting copy, as corrected by Faulkner and his editors, shows only minor dis-

---

[1] *An Exhibition of Manuscripts* (Texas), p. 13.

[2] *Faulkner in the University*, p. 76. [Frederick L. Gwynn and Joseph L. Blotner, eds. (Charlottesville: University of Virginia Press, 1959). Ed.]

[3] Reproduced in *The Book Collector*, IV (Winter 1955), facing p. 279.

crepancies from the published text, but it is interesting to see that it was only at a fairly late stage that Faulkner made up his mind about the conclusion of Chapter III. The typescript originally had Wash Jones tell Rosa to hurry out to Sutpen's Hundred, but Faulkner later added in holograph an ending similar to the present conclusion of Chapter IV, in which Wash tells Rosa that Henry has shot Charles Bon, only to opt finally for further suspension, striking the whole ending through and substituting the one which now appears on page 87 of the published book.[4] The main interest of the typescript is the evidence it provides of the extent to which Faulkner revised the book in response to editorial objections. There are also at Virginia a number of typescript pages from a version of Chapter I which preceded the version in the setting copy, and it is clear from annotations made on the first page that this version was at one time submitted as the first chapter of the final typescript. It is also clear that the pages missing from this rejected version were in fact incorporated into the final typescript, and it appears that while Faulkner was reworking the first chapter at his editors' request the printers went ahead and set up in dummy the first ten pages of Chapter II.

Comparison of the two versions of the first chapter shows that Faulkner reworked it in considerable detail. He retained many of the passages which the editors proposed to exclude, but he seems to have accepted other deletions and to have done a certain amount of re-writing, partly of passages to which the editors had raised some objection and partly of passages with which he himself was dissatisfied in some way.[5] Even where he did alter or delete passages to which his editors had objected, it is hard to believe that Faulkner accepted the reasons they advanced: the complaint, for example, that certain paragraphs contained material which the reader would be told about in greater detail later in the book was one which revealed little understanding of what Faulkner was trying to do in the novel as a whole. To comments about the content of the book Faulkner sometimes wrote a succinct and pointed reply. When an editor deleted a passage on the grounds that knowing Sutpen's father wouldn't have encouraged anyone to sign a note for Sutpen, Faulkner wrote: "It would in the South. If they had known who his father was, more than Compson

[4] Typescript setting copy, Alderman Library, p. 102.

[5] For Faulkner's retention of a passage, compare p. 9 of rejected version (reproduced in Fig. 14 of *Literary Career*) with p. 13 of the published book; comparison of the same two pages shows that in response to an editorial complaint that it was confusing to have a "musing" ghost Faulkner actually intensified the stylistic and syntactical extravagance of the passage. For still another version of the first chapter, see "Absalom, Absalom!" *American Mercury*, XXXVIII (August, 1936), 466–474; the chapter was published as one of a number of excerpts from work in progress by American writers. [James B. Meriwether, *The Literary Career of William Faulkner* (Princeton, N.J.: Princeton University Press, 1961). Ed.]

and Coldfield would have appeared to get him out of jail. *Leave as is.*" ⁶ Chapter I, however, is the only one which bears indications of extensive revision by Faulkner himself. Throughout the remainder of the book there occur editorial alterations which Faulkner apparently accepted without protest, perhaps in the interests of getting the book into print with the minimum of delay and distraction: it was his first novel with his new publishers, Random House, and he seems to have been prepared to make cooperative gestures which were unusual for him, at least at this stage of his career. These alterations consist mainly of minor deletions, additions of clarifying words or phrases, substitutions of proper names for pronouns, and rearrangements both of structures within sentences and of long sentences into shorter ones. There is, however, a marked decrease in the incidence of such alterations as the book proceeds, and from the latter part of Chapter VII to the end of the final chapter editorial marks of any kind are rare. A spot check revealed slight discrepancies between these portions of the setting copy and the published book, and these may represent alterations made at galley stage.

Whatever the state of the *Absalom, Absalom!* material may have been at the time Faulkner turned aside to write *Pylon,* it is clear from *Pylon* itself, and especially from its final pages, with their emphasis on the instability and malleability of fact, that the central technical and thematic problems of *Absalom, Absalom!* had continued to be very much in Faulkner's mind. The nature of these problems was well brought out in an exchange during one of the class discussions at the University of Virginia:

Q. Mr. Faulkner, in *Absalom, Absalom!* does any one of the people who talks about Sutpen have the right view, or is it more or less a case of thirteen ways of looking at a blackbird with none of them right?

A. That's it exactly. I think that no one individual can look at truth. It blinds you. You look at it and you see one phase of it. Someone else looks at it and sees a slightly awry phase of it. But taken all together, the truth is in what they saw though nobody saw the truth intact. So these are true as far as Miss Rosa and as Quentin saw it. Quentin's father saw what he believed was truth, that was all he saw. But the old man was himself a little too big for people no greater in stature than Quentin and Miss Rosa and Mr. Compson to see all at once. It would have taken perhaps a wiser or more tolerant or more sensitive or more thoughtful person to see him as he was. It was, as you say, thirteen ways of looking at a blackbird. But the truth, I would like to think, comes out, that when the reader has read all these thirteen different ways of

⁶ Marginal note to typescript setting copy, p. 16 (reproduced in *Literary Career,* Fig. 14).

looking at the blackbird, the reader has his own fourteenth image of that blackbird which I would like to think is the truth.[7]

These remarks are very much to the point. We have already seen Faulkner—most notably in *The Sound and the Fury,* most recently in *Pylon*—exploring the question of the subjectivity of experience, the elusiveness of fact. From a technical point of view, the four sections of *The Sound and the Fury* might be said to represent four different modes of cognition; in *As I Lay Dying* the whole action ultimately exists in the minds of the various characters, and certainly our understanding of that action depends upon our ability to disentangle fact from bias, to apply a correction factor, as it were, and make allowance for the distortions inherent in each of the different viewpoints. But in all of Faulkner's novels which employ a multiplicity of viewpoints the "experience" of the novel includes both the fact and the bias, and also, what is especially important, the tensions we perceive in their relationship. This is particularly true of *Absalom, Absalom!,* where the explorations of the nature of truth are pursued by means of a technique which becomes itself the sustaining medium of the action and the chief vehicle of meaning. In the direct narrative sense, *Absalom, Absalom!* is Sutpen's story: it is he who dominates the action, it is his tragedy which Quentin and Streve strive to recreate. Yet Sutpen, long dead, is reflected in such varied and usually violent shapes in so many different minds that he assumes an air of portentousness and mystery which, while fascinating Quentin and Shreve, makes him at the same time essentially unknowable. Sutpen, in fact, remains elusive both as symbol and as character. But what we do know about him is his meaning for, and effect upon, Quentin, and as the action progresses Sutpen recedes from the foreground, allowing the weight of the novel's major concerns to be subtly shifted onto Quentin's shoulders. By the end of the book the importance of arriving at a satisfactory interpretation of the Sutpen story is at least equalled by the importance of seeing the significance which this solution will carry for Quentin himself, the extent to which it will relax or tighten the rack on which he is stretched, the particular twist it will give to the knife.

It is fair to speak of the story as having three main narrators. Miss Rosa Coldfield and Mr. Compson are narrators in their own right, projecting distinct interpretations of Sutpen—interpretations deeply colored by the relationship in which they stand to him and by their own particular qualities of character and personality. The actual method or manner of their telling is also more distinct than has usually been allowed. Rosa's account, with its "demonizing" and

---

[7] *Faulkner in the University,* pp. 273–274.

linguistic extravagance, suggests the violence and verbal frenzy—action larger than life-size, language pushed beyond its proper limits—of decadent Jacobean drama:[8]

> *Once there was (they cannot have told you this either) a summer of wistaria. It was a pervading everywhere of wistaria (I was fourteen then) as though of all springs yet to capitulate condensed into one spring, one summer: the spring and summertime which is every female's who breathed above dust, beholden of all betrayed springs held over from all irrevocable time, repercussed, bloomed again. It was a vintage year of wistaria: vintage year being that sweet conjunction of root bloom and urge and hour and weather; and I (I was fourteen)—I will not insist on bloom, at whom no man had yet to look—nor would ever—twice, as not as child but less than even child; as not more child than woman but even as less than any female flesh. Nor do I say leaf—warped bitter pale and crimped half-fledging intimidate of any claim to green which might have drawn to it the tender mayfly childhood sweetheart games or given pause to the male predacious wasps and bees of later lust. But root and urge I do insist and claim, for had I not heired too from all the unsistered Eves since the Snake? Yes, urge I do: warped chrysalis of what blind perfect seed: for who shall say what gnarled forgotten root might not bloom yet with some globed concentrate more globed and concentrate and heady-perfect because the neglected root was planted warped and lay not dead but merely slept forgot?* (pp. 143–144)

Mr. Compson, on the other hand, much less involved, much cooler and more sceptical in his assessment of Sutpen and of the world at large, concentrates his attention on different aspects of the story and treats them in quite a different manner. His rather effete disenchantment suggests another form of literary decadence, that of the late nineteenth century, the *fin de siècle*,[9] and the sources and implications of his treatment of the Sutpen material appear quite specifically in his description of the octoroon's visit to Bon's grave:

> It must have resembled a garden scene by the Irish poet, Wilde: the late afternoon, the dark cedars with the level sun in them, even the light exactly right and the graves, the three pieces of marble (your grandfather had advanced Judith the money to buy the third stone with against the price of the store) looking as though they had been cleaned and polished and arranged by scene shifters who with the passing of twilight would return and strike them and carry them, hollow fragile and without weight, back to the warehouse until they should be

---

[8] Cf. comparison of *Absalom, Absalom!* with *The Atheist's Tragedy* in Anthony C. Hilfer, "William Faulkner and Jacobean Drama: A Comparison" (unpublished M.A. thesis, Columbia University, 1960), pp. 36–56.

[9] Cf. Ilse Dusoir Lind, "The Design and Meaning of *Absalom, Absalom!*," in *Three Decades*, p. 283; this reading of the novel is extremely interesting throughout. [Hoffman and Vickery, eds., *William Faulkner: Three Decades of Criticism* (East Lansing, Mich.: Michigan State University Press, 1960). Ed.]

needed again; the pageant, the scene, the act, entering upon the stage—
the magnolia-faced woman a little plumper now, a woman created of by
and for darkness whom the artist Beardsley might have dressed, in a soft
flowing gown designed not to infer bereavement or widowhood but to
dress some interlude of slumbrous and fatal insatiation, of passionate
and inexorable hunger of the flesh, walking beneath a lace parasol and
followed by a bright gigantic negress carrying a silk cushion and leading
by the hand the little boy whom Beardsley might not only have dressed
but drawn. . . . (p. 193)

The names of Wilde and Beardsley in this passage suggest that Faulkner is here making objective and dramatic use of that self-conscious
aestheticism which he himself had adopted during an early stage of
his career.

Miss Rosa and Mr. Compson have an essential role to play in the
total narrative structure; ultimately, however, the burden of recrea-
tion, interpretation, and suffering falls inexorably on Quentin, just
as, with utterly different effect, Mr. Lockwood is the final repository of
the story of *Wuthering Heights*. Shreve, Quentin's Canadian roommate at Harvard, participates in the task of imaginative reconstruction, but the final responsibility remains inescapably Quentin's. The
quotations from the narratives of Miss Rosa and Mr. Compson may
suggest that what confronts him is, among other things, a literary
task, virtually a problem of authorship, involving questions of literary
technique and of the author's attitude towards his material. This task
—a novelist's, perhaps, dealing in the creation of imaginative truth,
rather than an historian's—was the one which Miss Rosa, herself a
poet, had proposed for Quentin at the very beginning of the novel:

"So maybe you will enter the literary profession as so many Southern
gentlemen and gentlewomen too are doing now and maybe some day
you will remember this and write about it. You will be married then I
expect and perhaps your wife will want a new gown or a new chair for
the house and you can write this and submit it to the magazines. Perhaps
you will even remember kindly then the old woman who made you spend
a whole afternoon sitting indoors and listening while she talked about
people and events you were fortunate enough to escape yourself when
you wanted to be out among young friends of your own age."

"Yessum," Quentin said. *Only she dont mean that,* he thought. *It's because she wants it told.* (pp. 9–10)

Quentin's final failure to resolve the quasi-authorial problems which
confront him is closely related to his passivity, which itself has
important implications for his initial and much more successful role
of listener. It is the availability and apparent suitability of Quentin
as an audience which at once provokes and modifies the recitals of
Miss Rosa and Mr. Compson; the particular flavor of their narrations is largely determined by their awareness of who and what

Quentin is. As a young, intelligent Southerner, eldest son of his family and hence destined to become "the Compson," about to leave the homeland for the foreign environment of New England and Harvard, Quentin seems an appropriate repository for a story which they both dimly recognize as embodying some quintessential and symbolic relationship to the whole Southern experience, and which they both hand on to Quentin as if it were some dark inheritance from the Southern past. At the very beginning of the novel there are already two Quentins:

> Then hearing would reconcile and he would seem to listen to two sepa-
> rate Quentins now—the Quentin Compson preparing for Harvard in the
> South, the deep South dead since 1865 and peopled with garrulous out-
> raged baffled ghosts, listening, having to listen, to one of the ghosts
> which had refused to lie still even longer than most had, telling him
> about old ghost-times; and the Quentin Compson who was still too young
> to deserve yet to be a ghost, but nevertheless having to be one for all
> that, since he was born and bred in the deep South the same as she
> was—the two separate Quentins now talking to one another in the
> long silence of notpeople, in notlanguage, . . . (p. 9)

As the book proceeds, Quentin is buffeted to and fro not only between these two facets of himself but between the conflicting allegiances to differing interpretations of Sutpen and his story which seem to be demanded of him by Miss Rosa, by his father, and by the information he is able to collect for himself from other sources. His own version of the story contains, suspended in uneasy coexistence, substantial elements of all these interpretations, each of which attracts him for different reasons at different times. He never manages to free himself from these presences to the extent that would permit a radical re-interpretation of the whole Sutpen story and its Southern context, and he remains to the end that fatally divided and ghost-dominated personality to whom we are introduced at the beginning of the book:

> his very body was an empty hall echoing with sonorous defeated names;
> he was not a being, an entity, he was a commonwealth. He was a bar-
> racks filled with stubborn back-looking ghosts. . . . (p. 12)

In the later chapters of the novel, Shreve's participation in the reconstruction of Sutpen's story serves neither to remove from Quentin any of the final responsibility for the task nor to mitigate Quentin's anguish. For the most part Quentin and Shreve are seen as two young men, of similar age and aspirations, sharing intimately in the same experience of Harvard. Shreve is not presented as wiser than Quentin, nor as fundamentally unlike him; Shreve even races ahead of Quentin at times in his eagerness to give an essentially romanticized interpreta-tion of the relationships between Charles Bon, Henry Sutpen, and Judith (as at the end of Chapter VIII), and the two of them are caught

up together in their imaginative identification with the dead figures
of Henry and Charles—though it is significant that Quentin identifies more readily with Henry, the brother of Judith, and Shreve with
Charles Bon, the stranger to the world of Jefferson and Sutpen's
Hundred. Yet Shreve is not always precisely attuned to Quentin's
mood; indeed, he often cuts directly across it. At times he reminds
Quentin of Mr. Compson, and his attitude, though less cynical and
world-weary, is scarcely less sceptical. Faulkner once spoke of Shreve
as holding Quentin's story "to something of reality. If Quentin had
been let alone to tell it, it would have become completely unreal. It
had to have a solvent to keep it real, keep it believable, creditable,
otherwise it would have vanished into smoke and fury." [10] This is un-
doubtedly one aspect of Shreve's role; another is his contribution of
those moments of disenchanted humor which do something to relieve
the tension and actual pain of the final chapters. Moreover, the
presence of Shreve allows Faulkner to organize his material about a
dialogue, his favorite device for the treatment of direct narrative.
The relationship within the dialogue, however, is not simply that
of speaker and listener, as it was when Quentin was hearing the
accounts of Miss Rosa and Mr. Compson. Here the listener as a distinct,
passive entity almost disappears; what remains is the listener as constant *provocateur*[11] and as occasional brake—" 'wait then,' Shreve said.
'For God's sake wait.' " (p. 216) Shreve elicits from Quentin more and
more details of the Sutpen story. He deploys his rather aggressive ignorance about the South in such a way as to compel Quentin to face
difficulties which he might otherwise have passed over, and by his
relentless questioning at the very end of the novel—" 'Why do you
hate the South?' " (p. 378)—he forces Quentin to squeeze from the
story, and from himself, the last drop of anguish.

Only by death, it seems, will Quentin succeed in exorcising the
Southern ghosts which inhabit his body and mind, but the inter-
rogation by the alien Shreve in the alien New England climate and
situation at least brings Quentin to a fuller knowledge both of himself
and of his region. Quentin had been brought up to think of Sutpen
as probably a monomaniac and monster and as certainly an upstart
and a danger to the established social order; but as the story develops
Sutpen gradually assumes in Quentin's mind the shape and proportions of a tragic hero—a man of great personal power and splendid
vision; a bold seeker after those material values which all the South,
and all America, tacitly accepted as good, indeed as the essential
criterion of "quality"; a brave fighter and leader in the struggle

[10] *Faulkner in the University*, p. 75.
[11] Cf. Faulkner's comment on the role of the short convict in *The Wilds Palms* in
Faulkner in the University, p. 179.

against the North; and ultimately a defeated and tragic figure only because of his rigid adherence to principles of racial and social inhumanity which many besides himself were pledged to uphold. Quentin, as Faulkner remarked in a letter to Malcolm Cowley, must have thought of Sutpen as "trash." [12] What he learns is that in vigor, in character, and in vision Sutpen far outstripped any of Quentin's own family, alive or dead, and that Sutpen's history—his somewhat suspect purchase of the land from its Indian owners, his erection of a plantation and a great house at the cost of the sweat of his Negro slaves, his determination to found a dynasty—was only an exceptionally rapid and concentrated version of the history of virtually all Southern families, including Quentin's own. The point is explicitly made in the course of Miss Rosa's narration in Chapter V:

> *Judith created by circumstance (circumstance? a hundred years of careful nurturing, perhaps not by blood, not even Coldfield blood, but certainly by the tradition in which Thomas Sutpen's ruthless will had carved a niche) to pass through the soft insulated and unscathed cocoon stages: bud, served prolific queen, then potent and soft-handed matriarch of old age's serene and well-lived content—Judith handicapped by what in me was a few years' ignorance but which in her was ten generations of iron prohibition, who had not learned that first principle of penury which is to scrimp and save for the sake of scrimping and saving, . . .*
> (p. 156)

The implication for Quentin himself is clearly that those traditions and genealogies by which Southern families set such store—and not least the Compson family itself—were ultimately lacking either in substance or in value. What Quentin also learns is that the fatal flaw in Sutpen's design was precisely that flaw of man's inhumanity to man inherent in the recent history and structure of the South, a flaw represented not only by slavery itself but by other and surviving forms of racial and social intolerance.

One of the two most powerful images of such inhumanity in the novel is Sutpen's refusal to recognize Charles Bon as his son, with its bitterly ironic echo of that incident in his own childhood when he had been turned away from a door which he had counted on entering. The other image—even more vivid, perhaps, because more directly presented—is that of Sutpen's treatment of Milly Jones, the incident which directly provokes his murder at the hand of Wash Jones, Milly's grandfather. At the end of a life of devotion and unqualified admira-

[12] Faulkner to Cowley, 4: "[Quentin] grieved and regretted the passing of an order the dispossessor of which he was not tough enough to withstand. But more he grieved the fact (because he hated and feared the portentous symptom) that a man like Sutpen, who to Quentin was trash, originless, could not only have dreamed so high but have had the force and strength to have failed so grandly."

tion both of Sutpen and of those Southern values for which he appeared to stand, Wash Jones is brought to an appalled recognition:

> *Better if his kind and mine too had never drawn the breath of life on this earth. Better that all who remain of us be blasted from the face of it than that another Wash Jones should see his whole life shredded from him and shrivel away like a dried shuck thrown onto the fire. . . .* (pp. 290–291)

That it is not Sutpen alone who falls under Wash's condemnation but all Southerners of the class to which he now belongs, is made clear by Wash's allusions to the men he knows will shortly come to exact vengeance for Sutpen's death:

> men of Sutpen's own kind, who used to eat at his table with him back when he (Wash) had yet to approach nearer the house than the scuppernong arbor—men who had led the way, shown the other and lesser ones how to fight in battles, who might also possess signed papers from the generals saying that they were among the first and foremost of the brave—who had galloped also in the old days arrogant and proud on the fine horses about the fine plantations—symbol also of admiration and hope, instruments too of despair and grief; . . . (p. 289)

There are phrases here which eloquently evoke the tragic paradox of the old South as well as the agonizing ambiguity of the new valuation which Quentin as well as Wash Jones is forced to make: "symbol[s] also of admiration and hope, instruments too of despair and grief." Once Sutpen's situation begins to be properly understood, however, his ardent and valiant participation in the Civil War—that element in his character which Rosa Coldfield and, at first, Quentin himself find difficult to assimilate into their total conceptions of him—becomes entirely natural and indeed inevitable. Given his "design," his determination to acquire for himself all those advantages, actual and symbolic, which he had as a child identified as the essential possession of the rich and powerful, it is wholly understandable that he should be foremost among those who fought to preserve the particular system of society which alone upheld—economically, politically, and morally—the way of life to which he aspired and which, by the outbreak of the war, he had in fact attained. It is notable, however, that after the war he finds himself at odds with the more established representatives of his new class because of his refusal to join in anti-Reconstruction activities, rejecting what he apparently regards as the negativism of such activities in favor of more positive efforts to restore the land.

Sutpen remains in many ways a characteristic type of the *nouveau-riche*. One thinks, for example, of the ostentatious extravagance of his house and its furnishings, of the grandiose memorials which he obtains for his wife and himself at a moment of such desperate crisis for the

South, of the empty social posing of his wife. Ellen's attempt to secure Bon as a husband for Judith seems characteristic of the tendency of the *nouveaux-riches* to seek alliances with the old aristocracy, or at least with embodiments of the social graces which they feel themselves to lack. The story of Sutpen, considered simply as a social phenomenon, has a range of reverberation extending far beyond the limitations of its Southern setting—as does the human tragedy of Sutpen, with its suggestions of hubris and family doom on the Greek pattern.[13]

The point of departure for Sutpen's story—the image of the child being turned away from the big house, what is referred to in the novel as the "boy-symbol"—seems to have existed in Faulkner's imagination long before he began work even on his first attempt towards what eventually became *Absalom, Absalom!*. Among the Faulkner papers preserved at the University of Virginia is the typescript of an unpublished short story, "The Big Shot." The typescript is undated, but it is clear from the short story sending schedule which Faulkner kept at this time that he began sending it to magazines before January 30, 1930, and that it had already been rejected by four magazines before Faulkner sent it to the *Saturday Evening Post* on April 14, 1930.[14] In this early story there appears, as the central character, the figure of a racketeer called Dal Martin, operating in a Southern city during the Prohibition era; in the account which we are given of Martin's birth and history we see clearly, for all the disparity in time, the outlines of Thomas Sutpen, at least insofar as Sutpen spends his life "trying to get even with that man who in his youth had said, Go to the back door."[15] Martin, the narrator tells us,

> was born and raised on a Mississippi farm. Tenant farmers—you know: barefoot, the whole family, nine months in the year. He told me about one day his father sent him up to the big house, the house of the owner, the boss, with a message. He went to the front door in his patched overalls, his bare feet: he had never been there before; perhaps he knew no better anyway, to whom a house was just where you kept the quilt pallets and the corn meal out of the rain (he said "outen the rain"). And perhaps the boss didn't know him by sight; he probably looked exactly like a dozen others on his land and a hundred others in the neighborhood.
>
> Anyway the boss came to the door himself. Suddenly he—the boy—looked up and there within touching distance for the first time was

---

[13] Cf. Lind, op. cit., p. 281; Vickery, *The Novels of William Faulkner*, pp. 89–90. Evelyn Roddey Taylor, "A Comparative Study of Hawthorne and Faulkner" (unpub. M.A. thesis, Drake University, 1960), points to resemblances between *Absalom, Absalom!* and *The House of the Seven Gables* and between both of these works and the *Agamemnon* of Aeschylus (see especially, pp. 43–52, 108). See also Lennart Björk, "Ancient Myths and the Moral Framework of Faulkner's *Absalom, Absalom!*," *American Literature*, XXXV (May, 1963), 197–199.

[14] *Literary Career*, p. 170.

[15] *Faulkner in the University*, p. 73.

the being who had come to symbolize for him the ease and pleasant ways of the earth: idleness, a horse to ride all day long, shoes all the year round. And you can imagine him when the boss spoke: "Don't you ever come to my front door again. When you come here, you go around to the kitchen door and tell one of the niggers what you want." That was it, you see. There was a negro servant come to the door behind the boss, his eyeballs white in the gloom, and Martin's people and kind, although they looked upon Republicans and Catholics, having never seen either one, probably, with something of that mystical horror which European peasants of the fifteenth century were taught to regard Democrats and Protestants, the antipathy between them and negroes was an immediate and definite affair, being at once biblical, political and economic: the three compulsions—the harsh unflagging land broken into sparse intervals by spells of demagoguery and religio-neurotic hysteria—which shaped and coerced their gaunt lives. A mystical justification of the need to feel superior to someone somewhere, you see.

He didn't deliver the message at all. He turned and walked back down the drive, feeling the nigger's teeth too in the gloom of the hall beyond the boss' shoulder, . . .[16]

As a result of his experience Martin conceives an "unflagging dream" which he pursues by getting into favor with the boss—whom he finds himself not hating but admiring: "his folks would think he ought to hate him and he knew he couldn't!"—and, when the boss is in his dotage, drinking and playing cards with him behind the store. He eventually gains possession of the store, by means not entirely honest, sells it, comes to town with his wife and infant daughter, and sets up as a bootlegger. By the age of forty-eight he is a millionaire, living with his daughter in a large Spanish bungalow with an overlarge staff of Negroes, while his dead wife lies "beneath a marble cenotaph that cost twenty thousand dollars among the significant names in the oldest section of the oldest cemetary [sic]: he bought the lot at a bankrupt sale— . . . "[17]

The story itself has a somewhat arbitrary O. Henryesque ending and is not of especially high quality, but it is rich in elements which Faulkner was to take up and use in other stories and novels. We have already had occasion to note the presence in "The Big Shot" of Popeye, who reappears in *Sanctuary,* and Dr. Blount, who seems to bear a fairly direct relationship to Gail Hightower in *Light in August,* and there are even hints, in the treatment of the relationship between Martin and his daughter, of the Flem–Linda situation which Faulkner was to develop many years later in *The Town.* But the novel which draws most heavily on the story is obviously *Absalom, Absalom!,* and this indebtedness may provide some insight into a characteristic feature of Faulkner's creative method. He said at the University of

---

[16] "The Big Shot," typescript, Alderman Library, pp. 6–7.
[17] Ibid., pp. 10, 9, 13.

Virginia that for the writer the idea of a novel usually began "with the thought, the image of a character, or with an anecdote, and even in the same breath, almost like lightning, it begins to take a shape that he can see whether it's going to be a short story or a novel." [18] To such an initial image other material rapidly accreted, and in the process of writing a new novel Faulkner was very likely to absorb into it, perhaps in completely transmuted form, a good deal of diverse material which already existed in his memory or his imagination, or actually on paper—perhaps even published. It has already been suggested that some such process may have operated in bringing together the diverse strands of *Light in August,* which, according to Faulkner, began with the image of Lena Grove on her travels, and a similar accretion may have provided the material for *The Sound and the Fury* following the moment of Faulkner's realization that he wanted to write about the image of Caddy perched in the pear-tree. According to Faulkner, the starting-point of *Absalom, Absalom!* was Sutpen—"the idea of a man who wanted sons and got sons who destroyed him. The other characters I had to get out of the attic to tell the story of Sutpen." [19] It seems clear that in localizing and pinning down this somewhat abstract conception Faulkner took over several elements from the presentation of Martin in "The Big Shot," and notably the "boy-symbol" which was to become so important in the larger work.

Much of the material of "The Big Shot" is treated in a directly sociological manner, as befits the narrative point of view, which is that of an unidentified first-person narrator who is himself recording the story as it was told to him by a newspaper reporter named Don Reeves. *Absalom, Absalom!,* like all the novels of Faulkner's maturity, is grounded in a profound sense of social reality and of historical perspective, but its manner is diversified in accordance with the characterization of the participants in its multiple-narrative, all of whom claim to be concerned with truth, but none of whom, certainly, adopts a sociological or even reportorial approach. We have already pointed to the way in which Sutpen emerges as a type figure, both in terms of the history and society of the South and, as a successful entrepreneur and *nouveau-riche,* within a far broader context. But this view of Sutpen is built up piecemeal by the reader rather than presented directly by any of the narrators. Quentin, it is true, sees something of Sutpen's significance as a Southern figure, but until a late stage in the novel the presentation of Sutpen continues on the note and at the pitch set originally by Rosa Coldfield's "demonizing." It is Rosa's narrative, reinforced by the romantic tendencies evident

[18] *Faulkner in the University,* pp. 48–49.
[19] *Faulkner in the University,* p. 73.

in the imaginative reconstructions by Quentin and Shreve, which is primarily responsible for that aspect of the novel which has often led to the whole book being characterized as "gothic." That the term itself did not dismay Faulkner may be inferred from a remark he once made about Melville and which is also revealing of his attitudes towards his own work: "I think that the moment in the book, the story, demands its own style and seems to me just as natural as the moment in the year produces the leaves. That when Melville becomes Old Testament, biblical, that seems natural to me. When he becomes gothic, that seems natural to me, too, . . ." [20] The diversification of style in *Absalom, Absalom!* functions in just these terms.

The gothic characteristics of *Absalom, Absalom!* are worth investigating a little further, however, if only because they are among those features of Faulkner's work which have led critics to claim him as the major twentieth-century representative of American romance, inheritor of the tradition of Brockden Brown, Hawthorne, and Melville.[21] The similarities between Faulkner and Hawthorne have been frequently explored, and there have even been suggestions of specific resemblances between *Absalom, Absalom!* and *The House of the Seven Gables*.[22] There is, indeed, little doubt that Faulkner knew something of Hawthorne's work, and he includes him, along with Twain, Melville, and James, among those "predecessors who were the masters from whom we learned our craft." [23] But Faulkner included in the same list a number of English writers—Dickens, Fielding, Thackeray, Conrad, and Smollett—and he many times spoke of his debt to European authors such as Cervantes, Flaubert, Balzac, Chekhov, Gogol.[24] Faulkner's familiarity with English and European literature has often been ignored or underestimated by American critics, and the result has sometimes been not simply a misunderstanding of the nature and sources of many of his images and allusions but an insufficiently generous conception of the whole scale and direction of his endeavor.

If *Absalom, Absalom!* has gothic elements in common with *The House of the Seven Gables,* it shares far more with a novel like *Jane Eyre*. In both books there are major images of male power and one man (St. John Rivers in *Jane Eyre,* Sutpen in *Absalom, Absolam!*) who is iron-willed, immensely determined, and dedicated to the fulfillment

---

[20] *Faulkner in the University*, p. 56.

[21] See especially Richard Chase, *The American Novel and Its Tradition* (London, 1958), pp. 205–236.

[22] Taylor, loc. cit.

[23] *Faulkner in the University*, p. 243.

[24] See, for example, *Faulkner in the University*, p. 50, and cf. [Richard P.] Adams, "The Apprenticeship of William Faulkner," passim. [*Tulane Studies in English,* XII (1962): 113–56. Ed.]

of a purpose or design which is inhumane in its implications, against "life"—a man, as Jane Eyre says of St. John Rivers, who "forgets pitilessly the failings and claims of little people, in pursuing his own large views." [25] In each book there is a man whose first wife, a dark beauty from the West Indies, brings him wealth but has later to be put away for reasons of which the husband was unaware at the time of marriage: Sutpen's wife in *Absalom, Absalom!* because of the suspicion of Negro blood, Rochester's wife in *Jane Eyre* because she goes mad, although the presence of Negro blood is perhaps hinted at in Rochester's remark that his wife's family "wished to secure me because I was of good race; and so did she." [26] In each book the rejected wife continues to haunt her husband, threatening exposure and destruction. In each book, again, an unsophisticated girl is brought into a strange household and an important scene occurs in which the same young woman refuses what she considers an improper offer: Rosa Coldfield refuses to enter into an experimental liaison with Sutpen, while in *Jane Eyre* there is Jane's refusal to live with Rochester and also her refusal to marry Rivers, realizing that he does not love her but wants her only, as Sutpen wants Rosa, in order to fulfill his design. In both books there are great houses with secret inmates (Rochester's wife, Henry Sutpen) and mysterious guardians (Grace Poole, Clytie), and these houses are eventually set on fire by desperate women who themselves perish in the blaze.

This is not to suggest that Faulkner was deliberately engaged in writing an inverted *Jane Eyre*. Both novels are related to the gothic tradition, and many elements which they have in common are common also to the gothic pattern. Yet the resemblances are close, and it is tempting to think that Faulkner must at some time have read *Jane Eyre* and been deeply affected by it. The main point, at least, seems clear: that insofar as Faulkner resumes the gothic tradition in the novel he must be thought of as doing so from European sources quite as much as, or even more than, from native American sources. Faulkner may have felt some influence from Hawthorne, but the gothic of *The House of the Seven Gables* is lacking in the kind of uninhibited masculine violence which dominates *Absalom, Absalom!* and *Jane Eyre*. Among nineteenth-century American novels, only *Moby Dick* stands in this particular line, and there may indeed be traces of Captain Ahab in Faulkner's presentation of Sutpen; what is lacking even in *Moby Dick*, however, is the feminine perspective on masculine violence which characterizes Rosa Coldfield's narrative in *Absalom, Absalom!* and the first-person narrative of Jane herself in *Jane Eyre*.

The attractiveness of the analogy between *Absalom, Absalom!* and

[25] Charlotte Brontë, *Jane Eyre* (London, 1954), p. 414.
[26] *Jane Eyre*, p. 303.

Jane Eyre is increased rather than diminished by the fact that the complex organization of Faulkner's novel, the progressive piecing together of events and interpretations from the evidence provided by a variety of narrators, bears a certain resemblance to the structure of Emily Brontë's *Wuthering Heights,* a novel which Faulkner knew and "admired for its craftsmanship." [27] But in sheer intricacy of design *Absalom, Absalom!* goes far beyond *Wuthering Heights* or any other predecessor. One way of looking at the book's structure is to think of it as organized about a number of crucial moments of recognition, truth, disillusion: Henry and his father in the library, Henry shooting Bon, Sutpen proposing to Rosa, Wash Jones murdering Sutpen—each moment presented in a kind of tableau arrested at a particular point of time and held in suspension while it is looked at, approached from all sides, inspected as if it were itself an artifact, like that Grecian urn which Faulkner so often invoked elsewhere. The main business of the book then becomes the interpretation of these moments, the attempt to explain and make sense of them. Each moment is evoked again and again, and at each recurrence we seem to learn a little more about it and even to be moving towards a final clarification. Again and again, however, Faulkner stops us short of elucidation, constantly reinforcing in this way a suspense which, throughout the book, is created not so much by the withholding of narrative facts—almost all of these, indeed, are supplied in the opening chapter—as by the continual frustration of our desire to complete the pattern of motivation, of cause and effect. The movement of the book becomes almost wave-like—surging forward, falling back, and then surging forward again—and it is notable that most of the chapters, including the last, end on such moments of checked resolution.

Because he has spoken to Henry Sutpen,[28] Quentin possesses the

---

[27] *Faulkner in the University*, p. 202.

[28] See the arguments cogently advanced by John Hagan, "Fact and Fancy in *Absalom, Absalom!*," *College English*, XXIV (December, 1962), 215–218. Mr. Hagan's view that it was from Henry Sutpen himself that Quentin learned why he had shot Bon (not because of the octoroon mistress, nor because of the incestuous nature of his proposed marriage to Judith, but because of his Negro blood) receives further support from a passage which he does not quote: on p. 181 of the novel Quentin thinks that Shreve sounds *"just like father . . . Just exactly like father if father had known as much about it the night before I went out there as he did the day after I came back . . ."* The Chronology which Faulkner supplied for the novel provides additional evidence to show that Bon's Negro blood is one of the solid facts of the novel and not mere speculation on the part of Quentin and Shreve; against the year 1831, we read: "Sutpen learns his wife has negro blood, repudiates her and child." It is conceivable of course that the Chronology is unreliable as evidence, and it does contain two apparent errors. One of these, the dating of the visit of Rosa and Quentin to Sutpen's Hundred as 1910 instead of 1909, is apparently a simple, and understandable, slip. The other involves a more substantial discrepancy: on p. 210

vital piece of information, the fact that Charles Bon had Negro blood inherited from his mother, which "makes sense" of the most critical moment of all, the moment when Henry kills Bon. Yet for Quentin himself this rationalization constitutes the ultimate outrage: nothing for him is more appalling than the thought that the fratricidal tragedy, the monstrous end to a friendship and love which had promised to survive even the threat of incest (the obsessive theme of Quentin's section of *The Sound and the Fury*), should have been provoked by the ancient curse of the South. Shreve, with his utterly different background, cannot begin to comprehend the horror of this revelation, which Quentin must therefore face and come to terms with alone. Haunted by this knowledge, by his memory of the death-in-life of Henry Sutpen, and by the screams of Jim Bond, Quentin has at the end of the book found no relief: he lies, "his eyes wide open upon the window, thinking 'Nevermore' of peace. Nevermore of peace. Nevermore Nevermore Nevermore.'" (p. 373) For him at least the telling of the tragedy of Sutpen has brought no purgation or release.[29]

---

of the book we learn that Charles Etienne Saint-Valery Bon and Judith die of yellow fever; in the Chronology their death is ascribed to smallpox. That this was due neither to carelessness nor to a desire for ambiguity is suggested in "The Focus of William Faulkner's *Absalom, Absalom!*" (unpub. M.A. thesis, University of Virginia, 1959), p. 29, by Arlyn Bruccoli, who notes that in this instance Faulkner apparently used the Chronology to correct an error in the book. In *Absalom, Absalom!* (p. 210) Judith is said to have contracted the disease from Etienne and to have been buried apart as if it was feared that others might "contract the disease from her"; but yellow fever, Bruccoli observes, is not a contagious disease, although smallpox is, and it is perhaps worth adding that the manuscript version of the Chronology, now in the Alderman Library, simply records the deaths of Etienne and Judith without specifying the disease. Thus, while we may perhaps regret that Faulkner felt it necessary to supply a Chronology, there seems no reason to doubt its reliability as evidence.

[29] It is conceivable that in placing at this point the conclusion of Mr. Compson's letter, the first part of which appears just over 200 pages earlier (pp. 173–174), Faulkner intended to point towards the moment six months later when Quentin committed the suicide of which we have already learned from *The Sound and the Fury*. Mr. Compson, reporting the death of Miss Coldfield, observes:

> Surely it can harm no one to believe that perhaps she has escaped not at all the privilege of being outraged and amazed and of not forgiving but on the contrary has herself gained that place or bourne where the objects of the outrage and of the commiseration also are no longer ghosts but are actual people to be actual recipients of the hatred and the pity. (p. 377)

Mr. Compson is being his usual whimsical self, but for the ghost-tormented mind of Quentin his remarks might well have assumed a deeper significance, as offering, in fact, that solution and resolution which had so far proved elusive.

Absalom, Absalom!

by Melvin Backman

Seven years after the publication of *The Sound and the Fury* came *Absalom, Absalom!* (1936). *The Sound and the Fury* dealt with the fall of a family, *Absalom* deals with the fall of a society. The Quentin Compson of *Absalom* is not quite the same as the earlier Quentin: his concern is social rather than personal and his role is identified for the most part with a central quest in the novel—the quest to discover the truth about the rise and fall of his South. In its search for the truth about a whole society, the novel circles and shuttles back and forth in time, its sentences twist and strain, and its narrators attempt to re-create a past on the basis of some fact and much conjecture. Sometimes the narrators mislead unintentionally, sometimes they contradict one another, and often they are carried away by their own bias, preoccupation, or imagination. Admittedly, it is hard to come by truth, but still one might question whether a novel whose pitch is too shrill, whose approach is emotional and poetic, whose perspective seems unclear and shifting—one might question whether such a work presents the best way of getting at historical truth. The method of narration apparently mirrors not only the difficulty in getting at truth but the struggle to face truth. For all its straining, its complexities and obscurities, *Absalom*, I would conclude, is Faulkner's most historical novel.

Its intention, Ilse Dusoir Lind has said,

is to create, through the utilization of all the resources of fiction, a grand tragic vision of historic dimensions. As in the tragedies of the ancients and in the great myths of the Old Testament, the action represents issues of timeless moral significance. That Faulkner here links the decline of a social order to an infraction of fundamental morality cannot be doubted. Sutpen falls through innate deficiency of moral insight, but the error which he commits is also socially derived and thus illustrates the flaw which dooms with equal finality the aspirations of a whole culture.[1]

"Absalom, Absalom!" From Faulkner, The Major Years: A Critical Study *by Melvin Backman (Bloomington: Indiana University Press, 1966), pp. 88–112. Copyright © 1966 by Indiana University Press. Reprinted by permission of the publisher.*

[1] Ilse Dusoir Lind, "The Design and Meaning of *Absalom, Absalom!*," in Frederick J. Hoffman and Olga W. Vickery (eds.), *William Faulkner: Three Decades of Criticism*, p. 278.

For Mrs. Lind and most other critics, Sutpen is the South.[2] Yet some influential critics have qualified or contradicted this interpretation. Both Malcolm Cowley and Robert Penn Warren have stated in effect that "the Deep South was settled partly by aristocrats like the Sartoris clan and partly by new men like Colonel Sutpen." [3] Whereas they see Sutpen as only partly representative of the Deep South, Cleanth Brooks would question whether Sutpen is a Southerner at all. For Brooks, Sutpen is in many ways a Yankee: he "is a 'planner' who works by blueprint and on a schedule. He is rationalistic and scientific, not traditional, not religious, not even superstitious." "Indeed, Sutpen is at some points more nearly allied to Flem [Snopes] than he is to the Compsons and the Sartorises. Like Flem, he is a new man with no concern for the past and has a boundless energy with which to carry out his aggressive plans." [4] In seeing Sutpen as basically different from the other Yoknapatawpha planters and in associating him with the Snopeses, Brooks is making use of certain stereotypes that have been best described by George Marion O'Donnell:

> In Mr. Faulkner's mythology there are two kinds of characters; they are Sartorises or Snopeses, whatever the family names may be. And in the spiritual geography of Mr. Faulkner's work there are two worlds: the Sartoris world and the Snopes world. In all of his successful books, he is exploring the two worlds in detail, dramatizing the inevitable conflict between them.
>
> It is a universal conflict. The Sartorises act traditionally; that is to say, they act always with an ethically responsible will. They represent vital morality, humanism. Being antitraditional, the Snopeses are immoral from the Sartoris point of view. But the Snopeses do not recognize this point of view; acting only for self-interest, they acknowledge no ethical duty. Really, then, they are amoral; they represent naturalism or

---

[2] For example, Mrs. Vickery treats Sutpen as "a mirror image of the South," O'Connor as "the essence of the history of the South"; Howe regards *Absalom* as the "story of the fall of the homeland," Sullivan as the "complete statement of Southern ambition, execution and success, guilt, doom and destruction in one novel," Hoffman as "the vision of the South as a whole (or of human society itself) as a creation of this selfish and impulsive drive," and Waggoner as both "a lyric evocation of the Southern past" and "a search for the truth about human life as that truth may be discovered by understanding the past." See Olga W. Vickery, *The Novels of William Faulkner*, pp. 92–95; William Van O'Connor, *The Tangled Fire of William Faulkner*, pp. 94–96; Irving Howe, *William Faulkner: A Critical Study*, p. 161; Walter Sullivan, "The Tragic Design of *Absalom, Absalom!*," *South Atlantic Quarterly*, 50 (Oct., 1951), p. 560; Frederick J. Hoffman, *William Faulkner*, pp. 74–79; and Hyatt H. Waggoner, *William Faulkner: From Jefferson to the World*, pp. 149–153.

[3] This is Cowley's statement, which Warren paraphrases. See Malcolm Cowley, "Introduction to *The Portable Faulkner*," and Robert Penn Warren, "William Faulkner" in *William Faulkner: Three Decades of Criticism*, pp. 102 and 111 respectively.

[4] Cleanth Brooks, *William Faulkner: The Yoknapatawpha Country*, pp. 306, 307.

animalism. And the Sartoris–Snopes conflict is fundamentally a struggle between humanism and naturalism.[5]

Such a view—with its simplistic division of the South into Sartorises and Snopeses, its blindness to the guilt and tension and ambivalence which beset its Quentin Compsons—maps the reality neither of the historical South nor of Yoknapatawpha. It would, in fact, shut out reality and substitute legend; it would reduce the complexity of human life and character to a single abstraction. Contrary to the Sartoris–Snopes thesis, the antebellum South, though once ruled by the planter class, did not consist only of planter aristocracy and poor whites; the great majority of its people have always been hard-working small farmers,[6] like the Tulls and Bundrens and Houstons and Quicks and Armstids of Yoknapatawpha. Moreover, to attribute the decline of the South to the Snopeses is to compound legend with fantasy, for not only does such a view assume the existence of an aristocratic South based on a benevolent system of slavery and characterized by humanistic values but it finds a ready scapegoat for its ills in a tribe of Southern "Yankees," the Snopeses. It is more logical and just to assign the major responsibility for the fortunes of the South to its rulers—the Thomas Sutpens. And it is essential, if we are to understand *Absalom*, to know (1) the fact and legend of Southern history and (2) how Sutpen's life and career mirror the history and heritage of the South, moral as well as social and political.

Northern Mississippi was settled in the 1830s and 1840s. Mississippi did not become a state until 1817, and the town of Oxford, generally accepted as the prototype for Jefferson, was still an Indian trading post in 1835.[7] De Tocqueville, who travelled through America in the 1830s, described Southwestern society as "only an agglomeration of adventurers and speculators," [8] and Baldwin's *The Flush Times of Alabama and Mississippi* (1853) confirms de Tocqueville's appraisal. Historians generally agree that the Deep South, right up to the Civil War, was largely frontier country.[9] W. J. Cash, for example, describes the making of the great or Deep South in this manner:

[5] George Marion O'Donnell, "Faulkner's Mythology," in *Three Decades of Criticism*, pp. 83–84.

[6] Avery Craven, *The Growth of Southern Nationalism, 1848–1861* (Baton Rouge, Louisiana State University, 1953), p. 11; Avery Craven, *The Coming of the Civil War* (New York, Scribners, 1950), pp. 26–29; and Herbert Weaver, *Mississippi Farmers, 1850–1860* (Nashville, Tenn., Vanderbilt University, 1945), pp. 11–13, 28–29, 41, 48, and 57.

[7] Charles Sackett Sydnor, *Slavery in Mississippi* (New York, Appleton-Century, 1933), pp. 41, 247–248; and Ward L. Miner, *The World of William Faulkner* (Durham, N.C., Duke University, 1952), pp. 18–36.

[8] Alexis de Tocqueville, *Democracy in America*, ed. Phillips Bradley (New York, Knopf, 1946), I, 204.

[9] See, for example, Howard W. Odum, *The Way of the South* (New York, Mac-

1810 came and went, the battle of New Orleans was fought and won,
and it was actually 1820 before the planatation was fully on the march,
striding over the hills of Carolina to Mississippi—1820 before the tide
of immigration was in full sweep about the base of the Appalachians.

From 1820 to 1860 is but forty years—a little more than the span of
a single generation. The whole period from the invention of the cotton
gin to the outbreak of the Civil War is less than seventy years—the lifetime of a single man. Yet it was wholly within the longer of these periods,
and mainly within the shorter, that the development and growth of the
great South took place. Men who, as children, had heard the war-whoop
of the Cherokee in the Carolina backwoods lived to hear the guns at
Vicksburg. And thousands of other men who had looked upon Alabama
when it was still a wilderness and upon Mississippi when it was still a
stubborn jungle, lived to fight—and to fight well, too—in the ranks of
the Confederate armies.

The inference is plain. It is impossible to conceive the great South
as being, on the whole, more than a few steps removed from the frontier
stage at the beginning of the Civil War. It is imperative, indeed, to conceive it as having remained more or less fully in the frontier stage for a
great part—maybe the greater part—of its antebellum history.[10]

If this is so, who were the aristocrats of the Deep South? For the
great part, they were "but the natural flower of the backcountry grown
prosperous." [11] In Mississippi before 1860 a white man could lay claim
to the title of gentry if he acquired the land and the slaves. The importance of the established gentry of the Carolina, Tidewater, and
Natchez plantations lay not in their migration to the undeveloped
South but in the potency of their influence upon the South's lower
classes. Although some planters or their sons did come to the lower
South, most of the men pushing into the Mississippi wilderness were
from the backwoods. The plantation aristocracy served them as a symbol and goal, as the crown of a Southerner's achievement; it provided
the more successful and ambitious with a manner and tradition which
they put on, so to speak, like a new cloak. But after the Civil War the
South, "beset by the specters of defeat, of shame, of guilt," submerged
the fact and romanticized the claim of the planter.[12] Hence was
spread the legend of the Old South:

> the legend of which the backbone is, of course, precisely the assumption
> that every planter was in the most rigid sense of the word a gentleman.
>   Enabling the South to wrap itself in a contemptuous superiority, to

---

millan, 1947), p. 23; Vernon Lane Wharton, *The Negro in Mississippi, 1865–1890*
(Chapel Hill, University of North Carolina, 1947), p. 216; and Avery Craven, *The
Coming of the Civil War*, pp. 25–27.

[10] W. J. Cash, *The Mind of the South* (Garden City, Doubleday, 1954), p. 24.

[11] Ibid., p. 33. See also Frank Lawrence Owsley, *Plain Folk of the Old South* (Baton
Rouge, Louisiana State University, 1949), p. 90.

[12] Cash, p. 73. See also Craven, *The Coming of the Civil War*, pp. 17–18; and
Sydnor, *Slavery in Mississippi*, p. 248.

sneer down the Yankee as low-bred, crass, and money-grubbing, and even to beget in his bourgeois soul a kind of secret and envious awe, it was a nearly perfect defense-mechanism.[13]

Under the spur of the Civil War defeat, the Southerner's need to believe in the aristocracy of his ancestors and in the superiority of his tradition hastened the spread of the Southern legend. The legend affected the whole South, not just the Deep South. The force of its need and conviction submerged the fact that almost no members of the Cavalier aristocracy ever left England for America, that the Southern aristocracy derived from the low and middle classes, and that the aristocracy of the Deep South was made in one generation.[14] Scratch the veneer of the aristocrat of the Deep South and you would find a frontiersman. It was these new planters who took over the leadership of the Old South. The Natchez and Virginia gentry, longer exposed and hence more susceptible to the opinion of the rest of the Western world, were less able to conceive of slavery as a "positive good." But the new men brought to their position the frontier's aggressiveness, the strength and ruthlessness of self-made men, and a fierce faith in the righteousness of their cause and their interests. Nine-tenths of the men who directed the affairs of the Confederate government, like nine-tenths of the men who officered its armies, says Cash, were not Colonial aristocrats but new people.[15]

With the possible exception of Sartoris, all the founders of the ruling clans in Yoknapatawpha were new men. Sutpen, McCaslin, and Compson got their land by hook or by crook. Compson acquired his by swapping a mare to the Indians, Sutpen got his with a little Spanish gold, and McCaslin "bought the land, took the land, got the

---

[13] Cash, p. 73.

[14] Historians have long recognized that the Cavalier and planter legends derive from wishful thinking rather than fact. For early research on the subject, see Thomas Jefferson Wertenbaker, *Patrician and Plebeian in Virginia* (Charlottesville, privately printed, 1910), Preface and pp. 1–21 [Recent editions of his works have been published by Russell & Russell]; and G. W. Dyer, *Democracy in the South Before the Civil War* (Nashville, Methodist Episcopal Church, South, 1905), pp. 30–34. Although Wertenbaker established convincingly the non-aristocratic origins of the Virginia gentry, W. J. Cash, writing a generation later, had to explode the myth again. For other historical commentary, see Avery Craven, *The Coming of the Civil War*, pp. 17–34; C. Vann Woodward, *The Burden of Southern History* (Baton Rouge, Louisiana State University, 1960), pp. 12–13; and William R. Taylor, *Cavalier and Yankee* (New York, Braziller, 1961), pp. 17–18, 67, 96, 146–148, 203–205, and 334–341. The general acceptance of the Sartoris–Snopes interpretation of Faulkner's works suggests that the myth, in another form, still lives with us.

[15] Cash, p. 71. Avery Craven states: "A careful study of biographical materials and facts revealed in the manuscript census shows that only some 7.73 percent of the men who represented Virginia, the Carolinas, Alabama, Mississippi, Louisiana, Georgia, and Tennessee in the House and Senate from 1850 to 1860 were plantation owners or had come from families of plantation owners." Craven, *The Growth of Southern Nationalism*, p. 163.

land no matter how." [16] Faulkner has not told us how Sartoris got his land, but Sartoris possessed the "violent and ruthless dictatorialness and will to dominate" [17] which generally characterize the founders of the Yoknapatawpha ruling clans. The getting of the land, the hacking of a plantation out of the wilderness, and the establishment of a family dynasty would naturally promote violence, ruthlessness, and strength of character, and not "vital morality and humanism."

Nevertheless, Faulkner does make a distinction between Sartoris and Sutpen. They are different, not in the sense that Sartoris was an established Yoknapatawpha planter when Sutpen arrived at Jefferson in 1833—Sartoris did not arrive until a few years after Sutpen[18]—but in the sense that Sartoris's origin was "aristocratic" whereas Sutpen's was plebeian. Colonel Sartoris, as we see him in *Sartoris* and later in *The Unvanquished,* is a much more traditionally romantic figure than Sutpen. Sartoris, it is generally acknowledged, is modeled in part on the character and life of the author's great-grandfather, Colonel William C. Falkner. Yet Falkner's origin more closely approximates that of Sutpen than of Sartoris: Sartoris came to Mississippi "with slaves and gear and money" [19] from a Carolina plantation, but Falkner came out of Tennessee as a poor boy. The inference is plain: Sartoris represents in part a projection of the legend, but Sutpen represents the reality.

To get at the reality, however, would be difficult for Faulkner, difficult because he would not only have to work his way out of the distortions wrought by Southern legend and pride but he would have to repudiate the uncritical allegiance and assent demanded by a closed society even though it was still his home and native land. Yet the story, he said, "wouldn't let me alone"; he had to write it.[20] Next to *The Sound and the Fury, Absalom* was, admittedly, the novel that gave him the most trouble, the novel that apparently sprang out of compulsion and reluctance, out of pride and guilt, out of love and hate. The character in *Absalom* that expresses these ambivalent feelings is of course Quentin Compson. Without Quentin the story would never be told. He brings together all the facts and conjectures about Sutpen, he is the story's compelled listener and narrator, and he cares most about what Sutpen signifies.[21] "Out of the rag-tag and bob-ends of old tales and

[16] William Faulkner, *Go Down, Moses, and Other Stories* (New York, Random House, 1942), p. 256.

[17] William Faulkner, *The Unvanquished* (New York, Random House, 1938), p. 258. These words are voiced silently by Colonel Sartoris's son as he broods over his father's character.

[18] William Faulkner, *Requiem for a Nun* (New York, Random House, 1951), p. 44.

[19] Ibid.

[20] *Faulkner in the University,* ed. by Frederick L. Gwynn and Joseph L. Blotner, p. 281.

[21] Many critics have recognized that the Sutpen story is Quentin's story too, that

talking," [22] out of Miss Rosa's "demonizing" and his father's speculating, he must reconstruct a past that might have been, a man that apparently was. He must because the man in a sense was his ancestor, the past his past and present too.

The man, like almost all the aristocrats of the Deep South, began his life at the frontier. Most settlers of the South were descended from the English and "the half-wild Scotch and Irish clansmen of the seventeenth and eighteenth centuries," [23] and some of course came from the house of Old Bailey." [24] Thomas Sutpen was born in the mountains of west Virginia, his mother a Scottish mountain woman, his father an ex-prisoner of the Old Bailey. In the mountains "the land belonged to anybody and everybody and so the man who would go to the trouble and work to fence off a piece of it and say 'This is mine' was crazy" (221). At the frontier it was not possessions but physical strength that determined one's worth, the strength "to be measured by lifting anvils or gouging eyes or how much whiskey you could drink then get up and walk out of the room" (226). But at the mother's death the Sutpen family lost its hold upon their mountain home, "slid back down out of the mountains" (223), and "fell" (222) into a "land divided neatly up and actually owned by men who did nothing but ride over it on fine horses or sit in fine clothes on the galleries of big houses while other people worked for them" (221). That the journey from the highland to the lowland, from the democratic way of life of the frontier to the stratified plantation society of the Tidewater region was a fall is confirmed by the disintegration of the Sutpen family and the decline of their pride. The boy Thomas Sutpen saw his mother dead, his father transported in a drunken stupor, his brothers vanishing, his sister giving birth to two nameless bastards, and their home become a rotting cabin. In a futile attempt to

---

its full meaning does not make itself felt until the story has impacted upon Quentin's brooding, Hamlet-like conscience. The very tension between Quentin and what he is hearing and telling gives the novel its peculiar shading and significance. Faulkner himself has said that *Absalom* is both the story of Sutpen and "the story of Quentin Compson's hatred of the bad qualities in the country he loves" (*Faulkner in the University*, p. 71). A good analysis of this aspect of *Absalom* may be found in an essay by Richard B. Sewall, *The Vision of Tragedy* (New Haven, Conn., Yale, 1959), pp. 133–147.

[22] *Absalom, Absalom!* (New York, Modern Library, 1951), p. 303. All quotations from *Absalom* are from this edition.

[23] Cash, p. 42. See also Owsley, *Plain Folk of the Old South*, pp. 90–91.

[24] That Faulkner places little stock in the genealogical claims of Southerners may be inferred not only from the origins he assigns to Sutpen but from the words he puts into the mouth of Sartoris himself: " 'In the nineteenth century . . . genealogy is poppycock. Particularly in America, where only what a man takes and keeps has any significance and where all of us have a common ancestry and the only house from which we can claim descent with any assurance is the Old Bailey.' " *Sartoris* (New York, Harcourt, Brace, 1929), p. 92.

salvage something of their frontier pride the father whipped one of Pettibone's "niggers," and the sister sullenly refused to give way to a planter's carriage. But the unhappy transition from frontier independence to sharecropping subservience could not be effaced by violence against the Negro or by an occasional gesture against the planter. Now a man's worth was measured not by his manhood but by his possessions.

It was this humiliating truth that broke abruptly in upon the young Sutpen's innocence after the white door of the planter's mansion closed upon him and the "monkey nigger" told him to go around to the back. Retreating to a kind of cave in the woods, he brooded upon the meaning of this rejection. For the first time in his life he saw "his own father and sisters and brothers as the owner, the rich man (not the nigger) must have been seeing them all the time—as cattle, creatures heavy and without grace, brutely evacuated into a world without hope or purpose for them" (235). All that day he looked through his hurt into the face of the world's reality, until he knew that the only way to combat the world was to get for himself the land, the slaves, and the fine house upon which the planter had established his power and glory. He went to the island of Haiti to get what he wanted. He did not know that this "little lost island" (253) had been "manured with black blood" and "torn limbs and outraged hearts" (251). Like the single-minded Ahab, he knew only what he wanted. Crushing a slave rebellion, he rose from overseer to planter's son-in-law, and then to owner of land and house and slaves.

The decision that Sutpen made as a boy becomes the fateful decision of his life: he gave up the values of the frontier for those of a property–caste system. It was a decision full of bitter ironies, for in time it would lead to a war in which the backwoodsman fought by the side of the planter to preserve a system alien to his character and heritage. The planter and backwoodsman were separated by long-standing differences, but in the fierce mounting tension between North and South and in the War and its bitter aftermath, Southerners suppressed their differences. Still the union between planter and backwoodsman, despite its surface solidarity, remained fundamentally uneasy. Faulkner's own sympathies seemed to be on the side of the backwoodsman. Although Faulkner depicted the frontier way of life as crude and often brutal, he presented it as basically more honest and natural and innocent, simply because it was not founded on and sustained by property, by slavery. Ultimately, Sutpen's decision is a moral one: he committed the sin that would visit the iniquity of the father upon the children, and upon the children's children, unto the third and to the fourth generation. He did not know what he was doing, he would never know.

In 1829 Sutpen got his son. He named him Charles Bon—a name ironically reminiscent of Bonnie Prince Charlie, who was heir to a throne he never inherited and prince to a nation that repudiated him. In 1831 Sutpen repudiated his "Negro" wife and son. The repudiation of the Negro was compelled by the planter's "design." Yet the repudiation planted the seed of the system's destruction. Charles Bon represents both the doomed victim and fated undoer of the "design." He incarnates in a sense the tragic history of the American Negro. Running through his veins was the blood of the slavers and planters—the Spanish, French, English, and American—and the blood of the African Negro. But it was the Negro blood that would work like a strange power of fate in the lives of the planters, the slaves, and all their descendants.

Two decades after Columbus's discovery of the New World, Negro slaves were working in the sugar plantations of Haiti. Shortly thereafter Negro slavery spread to the mainland of America. The Renaissance and the Commercial Revolution had unleashed new energies and freedoms; one of them was "the freedom to destroy freedom." The enslaving and trading and working of Negroes were a principal means by which the newly powerful nation–states of Europe exploited the New World and filled their coffers. As Portugal, Spain, Holland, France, and England struggled in the next few centuries to expand their interests in the new hemisphere, the Negro slave became the pawn in the struggle. By the first quarter of the eighteenth century England was taking over most of the world's slave trade, and slavery was becoming a cornerstone in her economic prosperity. The West Indies, whose sugar plantations in the seventeenth century had been Britain's chief source of wealth in the New World, were now yielding their economic primacy to the mainland. In the American colonies, particularly in Virginia and the Carolinas, slavery continued to grow throughout the century. In the decade before the American Revolution, the colonists blamed the British crown for slavery. But, ironically enough, it was the United States, founded on and dedicated to equality and freedom, that became the arena for the greatest expansion of slavery the world had ever seen. Stimulated by a seemingly inexhaustible demand for cotton, which the Industrial Revolution had created, and enabled by Whitney's new invention to separate quickly the seed from the fiber, Southerners moved westward in search for new land to plant cotton. The southwestern lands were rich and ready to be taken. All that was needed was labor. Virginia, its soil exhausted by tobacco, had plenty of slaves and could in time breed more, and there were always the West Indies and Africa from which slaves could be smuggled into the United States. So was born the Cotton Kingdom.[25]

[25] John Hope Franklin, *From Slavery to Freedom* (New York, Knopf, 1952), pp. 42–183; and W. E. Burghardt Du Bois, *Black Folk: Then and Now* (New York, Holt, 1939), pp. 126–144.

Thomas Sutpen, who transplanted his slaves from Haiti to the Mississippi wilderness and transformed the wilderness to a plantation, was part of a large historical movement. He was part of the movement of slavery from the islands to the mainland and from the Eastern seaboard to the Southwest. Paradoxically, slavery was to find its most aggressive defenders in the Southern democrats of the United States. The very aggressiveness of the defense was related to various factors. For the Western world the nineteenth century was a century of industrial progress and intellectual liberalism, but for the South it was a century of resistance to the tide of liberalism and progress. Isolated, feeling itself threatened by a growing and hostile North, and harboring a bad conscience over its peculiar system, the South grew more ready to turn to violence. C. Vann Woodward, the Southern historian, has commented upon the South's state of mind immediately prior to the Civil War:

> The South had been living in a crisis atmosphere for a long time. It was a society in the grip of an insecurity complex, a tension resulting from both rational and irrational fears. One cause of it was the steady, invincible expansion of the free-state system in size and power, after the Southern system had reached the limits of its own expansion. The South, therefore, felt itself to be menaced through encirclement by a power containing elements unfriendly to its interests, elements that were growing strong enough to capture the government. The South's insecurity was heightened by having to defend against constant attack an institution it knew to be discredited throughout the civilized world and of which Southerners had once been among the severest critics. Its reaction was to withdraw increasingly from contact with the offending world, to retreat into an isolationism of spirit, and to attempt by curtailing freedom of speech to avoid criticism.[26]

"Much of the South's intellectual energy," Woodward continues, "went into a desperate effort to convince the world that its peculiar evil was actually a 'positive good,' but it failed even to convince itself. It writhed in the torments of its own conscience until it plunged into catastrophe to escape." [27] According to Woodward, the South, beset by a bad conscience, turned guilt and frustration into aggression and destruction. Woodward may be exaggerating the role played by conscience. We must remember that in the generation preceding the outbreak of the Civil War, the South was expanding: the frontier was being pushed westward and southward, the Cotton Kingdom was growing into the chief economic and social fact of the South's existence, and political power was shifting from Virginia and the Carolinas to the Deep South. The men who were making this expansion were caught up in the grip of their own ambitions and interests. They were passion-

[26] C. Vann Woodward, *The Burden of Southern History*, p. 62.
[27] *Ibid.*, pp. 20–21.

ate rather than reflective, doers rather than thinkers. Simply and fiercely they identified themselves and their interests with the South. Their proneness to violence was probably due less to bad conscience than to the fact that violence had played an important role in their frontier background and in their making of a plantation. It was a time when the South chose not a Thomas Jefferson but a Jefferson Davis as its leader. It was a time of Thomas Sutpens, not Quentin Compsons.

In the 1830s the men who would later become the leaders of the South in the Civil War were men on the make, men who had yet to achieve their dream. It was a "dream of grim and castlelike magnificence" (38) which Thomas Sutpen, with the help of his slaves and the captured French architect, built into the great house itself. With an assist from the puritan, Goodhue Coldfield, he acquired the appropriate furnishings for his baronial dream: the chandeliers, rugs, mahogany, and "the stainless wife" (51). The marriage of Thomas Sutpen to Ellen Coldfield signifies the union of frontiersman and puritan, a union which would give birth to the very character of the South. Frontier violence would be yoked to fundamentalist religion, frontier individualism would be wedded to the puritan's conscience. Superimposed on the marriage was the plantation system, with another set of values and with its Peculiar Institution.

In Mississippi the planter-to-be had no time to waste. Out of the virgin land Sutpen "tore violently a plantation" (9), and out of the virgin wife "without gentleness begot" (9) a son and daughter. He was hurrying his dream into shape. Even the names of his offspring and possessions reflect the dream. Charles and Henry might have come from English and Norman royalty, Judith from the Old Testament, Clytemnestra from the Greeks, and Rob Roy (his thoroughbred stallion) from Sir Walter Scott. By the 1850s Sutpen had become the biggest landowner and planter of Yoknapatawpha. "He acted his role too—a role of arrogant ease and leisure" (72), while his wife "moved, lived, from attitude to attitude against her background of chatelaine to the largest, wife to the wealthiest, mother of the most fortunate" (69). Dream had become actuality. "Now he would take that boy in where he would never again need to stand on the outside of a white door" (261). He had riven himself free from the brutehood of his past, made himself part of the proud and privileged class of the South, and had planted the heir who would perpetuate the achievement. So it seemed —until the Christmas of 1859 when retribution knocked on the white door of Sutpen's great house, and the past he had put away walked back into his life in the person of his first son, Charles Bon.

Charles Bon. Charles Good. In station and manners and breeding he was the elegant New Orleans scion, fortunate member of the planter class and an elite Latin culture. In personality he was "gentle sardonic whimsical and incurably pessimistic" (129). In his heart he was the son whose life had been "enclosed by an unsleeping cabal bent apparently on teaching him that he had never had a father" (313), he was "that mental and spiritual orphan whose fate it apparently was to exist in some limbo" (124), he was that "forlorn nameless and homeless lost child" (267) who came knocking on the white door of Sutpen's house. He wanted no inheritance; he wanted but a word, a sign, a look, a touch from Sutpen which would say you are my son. He got no acknowledgment, he got nothing. Even the love he got from his brother Henry turned into ashes when Henry learned that Bon was "the nigger that's going to sleep with your sister" (358). For all his sophistication, Bon remained only the orphan (he never really had a mother since, warped by paranoiac hatred of Sutpen, she had lost the power to love) who never found the father he sought: that was his fate. So it was that he lived as if something had gone out of him, as if he did not really want to live.

The story of Charles Bon is a richly ironic fable of the Old South. Bon embodies both the most favored of whites, a New Orleans scion, and the lowliest of blacks, the white man's bastard. He is the intelligent, cultivated young gentleman who must be shot by a Mississippi clod-hopper because the nigger signifies a subhuman threat to white woman-hood. Like his father, he cannot acknowledge his son by a colored woman. These ironies are part of a system; beneath these ironies rest others parts of the system's foundation. In the Old South the Negro slave had generally no father and little mother. Under a system that made human beings into chattels, the Negro woman, when she did not labor in the fields, served as the breeder of stock and as the instrument for the white man's sexual pleasure. The Negress was a kind of mare, the Negro a stud. The effect was to destroy or warp the institution of the family among a whole people. In removing sex from its familial role, the system did violence to the morality of both whites and blacks.[28] It made sex for the Negro into an irresponsible animal rela-tionship; it made sex for the white man into a guilty, dishonest one. A schism, a kind of unconscious hypocrisy, embedded itself deeply into the soul of the South. For the white man the Negress was the female

[28] It is of course difficult to appraise the moral and psychological damage done to the Negro in the process of enslaving him. One can suggest, however, some historians and commentators who provide information and insight: Frederick Bancroft, *Slave Trading in the Old South* (New York, Ungar, 1959); E. Franklin Frazier, *The Negro Family in the United States* (New York, Dryden, 1948); John Hope Franklin, *From Slavery to Freedom;* W. E. Burghardt Du Bois, *Black Folk: Then and Now;* Frank Tannenbaum, *Slave and Citizen: The Negro in the Americas* (New York, Knopf, 1947); Daniel P. Mannix, in collaboration with Malcolm Cowley, *Black Cargoes: A History of the Atlantic Slave Trade* (New York, Viking, 1962); Frederick Douglass, *Narrative of the Life of Frederick Douglass, an American Slave, Written by Himself,* edited by Benjamin Quarles (Cambridge, Belknap, 1960); and Stanley M. Elkins, *Slavery* (Chicago, University of Chicago, 1959).

animalized and the white woman was the female spiritualized. It was
as if the planter were trying to make up to his white woman for his
faithlessness and duplicity.[29] Reality was two families by the planter,
white and black. Reality was a brother who was not a brother, a sister
who was not a sister, a wife who was not a wife. Southerners knew of
this reality, accepted it, lived with it, even though it violated what
they thought they believed in: honor, pride, the family, and the de-
cencies of life. This reality underlies the story of the House of Sutpen.

All the relationships in the Sutpen family are invested with a peculiar irony, doom, and tragedy, as if a curse had been placed on them
like the curse of the House of Oedipus. Incest, fratricide, and the fall
of a family are all aspects of both curses. Moreover, like several characters in *Oedipus Rex,* the Sutpens, for the most part, did not know the
full truth about themselves and could not realize their identity and
humanity. Henry and Charles were brothers, yet not brothers; Judith
and Charles were sister and brother, yet not sister and brother; Sutpen
and Charles were father and son, yet not father and son. They seem
compelled as by a Greek fate—such is the power of the system—to repudiate or destroy one another; they seem compelled as by the Old
Testament God to suffer for the sins of their father. It was the father,
the nucleus of the culture, who determined the fate and character of
the others. He signifies an elemental force, a heroic *hybris,* in the
Southern culture; he is the archetype of the Southern planter. There
is a grandeur to the man who hammers out his "design" in the face
of God's and nature's opposition. Yet there is a fatal defect too: his
Adamic innocence, like that of other American barons on the make,
had hardened into moral blindness, and the egoism and energy gen-
erated by his rejection and dream of vindication had become ultimately a force for destruction of himself, his family, and his society.
In attempting to build a dynasty, he had lost a family; in making himself into the image of the Southern planter, he had lost part of his
humanity; in displacing conscience by pride, he had lost the power
to see into himself. Since he was "incapable of that rending of the
self and tearing out of pride which forms the tragic element," [30] his
life ended not in tragic affirmation but in gross deterioration and un-
heroic death.

Ironically, the lowliest of the whites is the instrument of retribution.
For Wash Jones the Colonel signified all that was best in the planter:
courage, honor, paternalism, and authority. For Wash the Colonel was
a god:

> . . . on the week days he would see Sutpen (the fine figure of the man
> as he called it) on the black stallion, galloping about the plantation, and
> Father said how for that moment Wash's heart would be quiet and

[29] See Cash, pp. 97–98.
[30] Howe, p. 164.

proud both and that maybe it would seem to him that this world where
niggers, that the Bible said had been created and cursed by God to be
brute and vassal to all men of white skin, were better found and housed
and even clothed than he and his granddaughter—that this world where
he walked always in mocking and jeering echoes of nigger laughter, was
just a dream and an illusion and that the actual world was the one
where his own lonely apotheosis (Father said) galloped on the black thoroughbred, thinking maybe, Father said, how the Book said that all men
were created in the image of God and so all men were the same in God's
eyes anyway, looked the same to God at least, and so he would look at
Sutpen and think *A fine proud man. If God Himself was to come down
and ride the natural earth, that's what He would aim to look like.* (282)

In spite of the blind contradiction in Wash's belief that the Bible
could be used as authority for both the Negro's enslavement and
man's equality, there is something touching about Wash's faith in the
planter who had sprung from the same brute origins but who in the
span of several decades had become the poor white's apotheosis. By
1869, however, the ravages of the War and Reconstruction had eaten so
deeply into the planter and his "design" that his power was being
broken and his ruthlessness exposed. The breaking point came when
Sutpen, having attended the mare that had just foaled a colt to his
stallion, entered Wash's cabin to see whether he had bred a son by
Milly, Wash's granddaughter. Bending over the pallet where she lay
with her newborn daughter, he said, " 'Well, Milly; too bad you're not
a mare too. Then I could give you a decent stall in the stable' " (286).
The earth seemed to fall away from beneath Wash's feet. He confronted the planter. Like the Grim Reaper, he raised the rusty scythe;
the planter's whip lashed twice across his face, and then the scythe
came down.

Although the poor white has been depicted as the instrument of the
planter's demise, the deterioration of Sutpen's will and character,
wrought by the inroads of the War and Reconstruction, contributed
also to his downfall. The planter's confidence and power had been
deeply shaken by the loss of the War; nevertheless, the Southern people
did not actually repudiate their leaders until much later. Toward the
end of the nineteenth century they did begin to turn to other leaders,
to those who made the Negro the scapegoat for the Lost Cause and
the current ills. The Negro, who had once been inviolate as the planter's chattel, became fair game for any white. Providing an outlet for
the people's frustration and resentment, racism became the official pol-
icy of the South. In effect, Faulkner was right: the poor white eventually did turn on the planter.

What survived from Sutpen's "design"? There was the heir apparent, Henry Sutpen, who vanished for a generation, only to reappear
at the beginning of the next century like a futile ghost out of a dead

but lingering past. And there were the three women: Judith, Clytie, and Rosa Coldfield. Judith had been intended *"by the tradition in which Thomas Sutpen's ruthless will had carved a niche to pass through the soft insulated and unscathed cocoon stages: bud, served prolific queen, then potent and soft-handled matriarch of old age's serene and well-lived content"* (156). Instead, she had become *"the bowed and unwived widow kneeling"* (138) beside her lover's corpse. She lived on in the empty and rotting house, scraping out a meager existence by doing a man's labor. In silent, stoic joylessness she survived the privations of the War and Reconstruction. Her mulatto sister, Clytie, continued long beyond Judith's death as the guardian of her master's house. Clytie represents the Negro family servant so involved with her white folks that she could make no life of her own. Finally there was Miss Rosa. Conceived in her parents' old age, as Gail Hightower had been, she passed from a warped childhood to a spinster's dream world and became a writer of odes to Confederate heroes. But the emotional thrust of her life derived from her hatred of Sutpen, a hatred which stemmed mainly from his matter-of-fact proposal "that they try it first and if it was a boy and lived, they would be married" (284). Faulkner's characterization of Miss Rosa is generally rendered in broad paradox and sly irony. She is both the chaste Southern woman and warped old maid; the romantic defender of the South and paranoiac hater of its supreme representative, Thomas Sutpen; vicarious bride in her dreams to Charles Bon and hater of the Negro. So shielded had she been from the realities of the Old South, Rosa Coldfield never knew she had loved the "nigger" son of Thomas Sutpen.

The true heir of the grand "design" was Charles Etienne Saint-Valery Bon, only child of Thomas Sutpen's elder son. Neither black nor white, living in a much less fortunate time and having less than his father, he became the classic mulatto pariah. He struggled to find his identity by marrying a coal-black woman and living a Negro's life; but he could only express himself by destroying himself, by "treading the thorny and flintpaved path toward the Gethsemane [sic] which he had decreed and created for himself, where he had crucified himself and come down from his cross for a moment and now returned to it" (209). "With a furious and indomitable desperation" (202) he flung the gage of his apparently futile challenge in the white world's face and turned from his "emancipation" to death.

As the nineteenth century yielded to the twentieth, there survived the rotting house, its slave guardian, the death-in-life heir (Henry), and the last Sutpen descendant—the idiot, Jim Bond. It had taken two generations for Bon to become Bond, good to become slave.[31] Not much was left of the planter's baronial dream. Like the planter's

---

[31] I am indebted to Konrad Hopkins for this idea.

mansion, the dream kept rotting. In December 1909 the house of Sutpen went up in smoke. Only the idot remained. The others were dead. Dead was the planter with his double family, black and white; dead were the Coldfields, with the shopkeeper's barren puritanism and the spinster's barren gentility; and dead was the poor white family of Wash Jones.

A mood of despair and futility pervades this story of the South. Even the most decent of men, General Compson, could only conclude when touched by the misery and destructiveness of Valery Bon's life, *"'Better that he were dead, better that he had never lived'"* (205). Yet the despair has been quickened by a kind of fierce, underground idealism. Valery Bon destroyed himself not only because he would rather be dead but because he felt compelled to make a protest against the system which denies his people their human rights. Even Wash Jones's life ended in protest. From an outraged and anguished heart Faulkner has cried out in *Absalom* against an evil implanted in his South.

Faulkner has presented Sutpen as the source of the evil, but he has presented him too as the only heroic figure in the story. Sutpen is both the pride and the shame of the South. For a Quentin Compson the ambivalence of his feelings about his heritage is further complicated by the reality of the present. His heritage is peculiarly compounded of accomplishment and defeat, innocence and guilt, pride and defensiveness. The ruthless planter–backwoodsman who built his house upon slavery and lived as if the evil were a positive good is dead and gone. For his descendants accomplishment has often become but a memory, pride has become delusion, and innocence has become unacknowledgeable guilt. As loyalty to the Old South has turned into savage racism, the planter's power to act has deteriorated for his twentieth-century descendants into a stasis of will.

For Quentin, as for his father, Sutpen represented another time when men were

> simpler and therefore, integer for integer, larger, more heroic and the figures therefore more heroic too, not dwarfed and involved but distinct, uncomplex who had the gift of loving once or dying once instead of being diffused and scattered creatures drawn blindly limb from limb from a grab bag and assembled. . . . (89)

Out of his sense of impotence and alienation, Quentin, like Bon himself, seemed to turn to the godlike Sutpen for the power and virility he lacked, for the father who would solve the son's dilemma. But the giant, rising out of the past like a swiftly growing djinn from Aladdin's lamp, threatened to consume rather than renew the puny summoner. The vision of the South which Quentin invoked left him shivering, "panting in the cold air, the iron New England dark; *I dont. I dont!*

I dont hate it! I dont hate it!" (378). Even in the alien air of New England the South was too much with him. The burden of its history lay heavy upon Quentin Compson. Torn by loyalty and guilt, by the desire to defend and the need to expiate, by the desire to suppress and the need to confess, he could only cry out against his burden. And this is how the novel ends—with the sins of the past unexpiated and the dilemma of the present irresoluble.

Absalom, Absalom!
The Extended Simile

by James Guetti

Absalom, Absalom! at first seems to be merely a puzzle. If, as is likely, we assume that novels are usually coherent and consistent, then the incapacities of the narrators who present the first and second accounts of Thomas Sutpen will appear to be temporary difficulties that will at last be solved. The confusing introduction to the story of Sutpen through Mr. Compson and Rosa Coldfield will be followed, we might suppose, by a more able narrator and by relative clarity and comprehension. We find, however, that the third of the principal narrators of the book, Quentin Compson, provides no simplification of the complexities we have encountered. Some of the supposed "facts" have been changed, to be sure, and Sutpen's experiences now appear to make better sense as a sequence of cause and effect. But the circumstances in which this last story is told, Quentin's drastically ambivalent attitude toward the value of his own remarks and perceptions, his relation to his account as it is described by the anonymous narrator, and the implications of that account all suggest that the inability of the narrators to understand the experience surrounding Sutpen may be an expression of a consistent theme: that human experience cannot be understood, that order cannot be created.

The view of the story presented by Quentin's father depends both upon a lack of information—or what a reader assumes, at this point, to be information—and upon the apparent demands of Mr. Compson's own sensibility. In his hands the story becomes not what happened but what, in the absence of certainty as to the facts, he would like to think happened. His narrative is constantly shown to be his own hypothesis as to what "must have been" and is always explicitly bounded by what he is able to imagine and what he prefers to believe.

Mr. Compson's remarks express a great many motives and actions that he cannot explain. And what he cannot explain he characteris-

tically redefines as what cannot be explained and then as evidence of
something he calls "chance." In attempting to understand Sutpen's
investigation of Bon, he remarks, "You would almost believe that
Sutpen's trip to New Orleans was just sheer chance, just a little more
of the illogical machinations of a fatality." [1] As may be noted here,
"chance" and "fatality" are closely associated, perhaps synonymous,
in Mr. Compson's mind and in his story. The movement toward an
insistence upon the operation of this chance–fatality is clearly exem-
plified in the following passage:

> . . . we see dimly people . . . possessing now heroic proportions, per-
> forming their acts of simple passion and simple violence, impervious to
> time and inexplicable—Yes, Judith, Bon, Henry, Sutpen: all of them.
> They are there, yet something is missing; they are like a chemical formula
> exhumed along with the letters from that forgotten chest . . . you bring
> them together in the proportions called for, but nothing happens; you
> re-read, tedious and intent, poring, making sure that you have forgotten
> nothing, made no miscalculation; you bring them together again and
> again nothing happens: just the words, the symbols, the shapes them-
> selves, shadowy inscrutable and serene, against that turgid background of
> a horrible and bloody mischancing of human affairs. (101)

All of Mr. Compson's important attitudes are present here: his inability to understand the story or even to appreciate the reality of the
characters; his concomitant sense of the story as "mischancing"; and
an assumption that seems to underlie it all—that these characters possessed "heroic proportions." It appears that Mr. Compson's insistence
upon the presence of the inexplicable in his narrative has a partial
source in his desire to view the Sutpens as heroes, that by presenting
them in conflict with a "fatality" he is able to lend them great stature.
In this way, what he cannot explain becomes sacred to him, and "they
don't explain" becomes "we are not supposed to know" (100). It is
as if he is aware that his view of the story as heroic tragedy depends
upon its remaining unexplained and that he is therefore reluctant to
pursue his inquiries.

Mr. Compson's heroic view, in fact, is unquestionably self-conscious:
"Fate," he suggests, is the "stage manager" (73), and the history of the
Sutpens is like a "Greek tragedy" (62). On the one hand, this explicit
labeling of his perspective draws our attention to the inadequacy of
the view itself, but on the other hand it is evidence of Mr. Compson's
own awareness that his understanding of the story arises from a stock
metaphor—the world as heroic stage—founded upon what he cannot
explain. It may be, in short, that Mr. Compson himself, as well as a
reader, is aware that his heroic past is as fictional as Greek tragedy
itself. His assertion of such a past will thus seem the result not of a

---

[1] William Faulkner, *Absalom, Absalom!* (New York: Random House, Inc., 1951),
p. 102. All subsequent references to *Absalom, Absalom!* are to this edition.

private compulsion but of a more balanced attempt to deal with a circumstantial lack of knowledge and vision.

Because of these limitations that are perhaps psychological and certainly circumstantial, a reader is acutely conscious of the artificiality of Mr. Compson's narrative. This same artificiality, however, seems evidence of a reality to come; Mr. Compson's failure, we suppose, is simply preparation for a speaker of greater imaginative flexibility and fuller knowledge. We imagine that *a* story about Thomas Sutpen will be told—some yet unrevealed story for which Mr. Compson's narrative is a momentary disguise and substitute.

But this more capable speaker is not Rosa Coldfield, for she, like her predecessor, may be seen to transform an inadequacy into a suspect virtue. Rosa continually reveals her feelings of amazement and her inability to make any sense whatever of the story, but at the same time she exhibits a fanatical certainty about it. As in the case of Mr. Compson, the certainty depends upon the inability, for by viewing Sutpen's story as inexplicable in terms of what she judges to be predictable human activity, she is able to insist that the man is superhuman. Sutpen becomes a "demon" who appears out of nowhere to enact an evil fatality:

> I saw Judith's marriage forbidden without rhyme or reason or shadow of excuse; I saw Ellen die with only me, a child, to turn to and ask to protect her remaining child; I saw Henry repudiate his home and birthright and then return and practically fling the bloody corpse of his sister's sweetheart at the hem of her wedding gown; I saw that man return— the evil's source and head which had outlasted all its victims—who had created two children not only to destroy one another and his own line, but my line as well, yet I agreed to marry him. (18)

Throughout her narrative Rosa insists that she was a passive observer and the victim of an outrageous fatality beyond her understanding. In the intensity of her failure to understand she declares that the story cannot be understood; she insists further that what is incomprehensible to her must be supernatural.

Rosa's understanding of the story, in other words, is inseparable from her feeling of outrage. She occasionally asserts that Sutpen's goal was "respectability" (16), and at another moment, she is sure that he is driven by "ruthless pride" and a "lust for vain magnificence" (162). These characterizations of Sutpen may be seen to depend upon Rosa's more personal concerns, upon her response to what may have been a proposal of a trial copulation. They depend upon her view of herself as the image of that respectability which Sutpen, in her terms, constantly offended and finally outraged.

It now becomes possible, once again, to see Rosa's narrative as we have seen Mr. Compson's: the narrative problem appears to be a defined psychological problem. But also like Mr. Compson, Rosa

Coldfield's supposed psychological difficulties are questioned by her own awareness of the way in which they work; she insists, in fact, upon the fallibility of her perspective: *"there is no such thing as memory: the brain recalls just what the muscles grope for: no more, no less: and its resultant sum is usually incorrect and false and worthy only of the name of dream"* (143). If we say that she sees what she wants to see, we must also admit that she knows that she is doing so.

The problem of perception, however, extends beyond the matter of memory, for Rosa often declares that the very past in which she lived and of which she speaks did not exist for her at the time. This feeling reaches its culmination when she describes Charles Bon, who is to her the most important figure of that past. She loved Bon, she says, with a love founded upon contradiction and paradox, *"beyond the compass of glib books: that love which gives up what it never had"* (149). She loved, as she remarks, a man who may not have ever existed at all except as her own imagined creation, a man she never saw alive or dead: *"That was all. Or rather, not all, since there is no all, no finish. . . . You see, I never saw him. I never even saw him dead. I heard an echo, but not the shot; I saw a closed door but did not enter it"* (150). What for her is the climax of the story that began with Thomas Sutpen's arrival in Jefferson is exactly that which is most anticlimactic, and what is most important to her is least real. And this was because, she tells us elsewhere, she was then *"living in that womb-like corridor where the world came not even as living echo but as dead incomprehensible shadow"* (162). Bon was unreal to her simply because he was somewhere outside that "corridor," beyond which even the commonplace might have been unreal.

Again as with Quentin's father, Rosa's self-awareness tends to modify a reader's conception of her limitations. If these limitations themselves make us aware of the fictional quality of her narrative, her confession of them suggests that her problem is not largely "psychological" nor even definitely emotional. This feeling is corroborated later when we learn that her sense of outrage and amazement has a more significant source than the insulting of her virginal and respectable self-conception; *"for almost fifty years"* Rosa has asked of Sutpen's second proposal, *"Why? Why? and Why?"* (167). Whereas before her inability to comprehend the experience of which she tells seemed to be the product of a lesser, simply old-maidish outrage, at this point her failure appears the result of a genuine, even desperate attempt to understand.

In both the case of Mr. Compson and that of Rosa, then, internal, psychological difficulties seem less important than the sheer external facts of their situations. Rosa's awareness of her failure deflects the emphasis from a supposed neurosis within her to something acting upon her from without—a "corridor," a set of limitations which she somehow cannot escape. The emphasis upon circumstances in her case, it appears, is even greater than for Mr. Compson.

A reader may assume even now, however, that *Absalom, Absalom!* is a novel like other novels, that a story exists and will be told. No matter how circumstantial the narrative insufficiencies of Quentin's father and Rosa Coldfield may seem, as insufficiencies they are inseparable from the characters themselves, and we continue to expect a better speaker; the narrative difficulties, we suppose, are still difficulties that the last character–narrator of the novel—Quentin Compson— will not have.

Both Rosa and Mr. Compson are present in the story that Quentin tells. While the long, frequently interrupted dialogue with Shreve in a room at Harvard is always subject to his modification and approval, the narrative that it comprises is an amalgamation of the narratives of many: General Compson, Mr. Compson, Rosa, Shreve, and of course Quentin himself.[2] This section of the novel, that is, contains narrative matter and techniques that we recognize, and both Shreve and Quentin are aware, more specifically, that they sound like "father."

One aspect of Quentin's own particular method, however, is immediately apparent. In the narratives of Rosa and his father it is the limitations of these speakers that are initially most striking and most revealing, but Quentin's story is different. For the first time in the novel a reader is presented with a powerfully imagined narrative that—no matter how much it may be questioned ultimately nor how puzzling its arrangement—is in general consistent and reasonable within itself.

Quentin's relation to the story he tells is often characterized as that of direct perception: "It seemed to Quentin that he could actually see" (132). This remark is on occasions simply repeated verbatim, on others slightly modified. And at times it serves to introduce a narrative of startling imaginative intensity, as, for example, when Henry Sutpen and Bon confront each other on an approach to Sutpen's Hundred, one brother about to destroy the other. Considering that Quentin is frequently described as a seer, that he has moments of clarity that other narrators do not have, and that the story he tells seems to work as a story, he appears to be the narrator we have been awaiting, who will endow the story with meaning and imaginative reality.

It is necessary to notice, however, that it only *seems* to Quentin that he can see. The limitation that begins here in the word "seems" grows larger when we consider that Quentin is often described as exhibiting a quality that is generally antithetical to his supposed imaginative

---

[2] Because this "dialogue" is always subject to Quentin's approval, we may for the sake of economy of reference consider it as a unified section of the narrative. In my discussion, also, I rely much more upon Quentin's remarks than upon Shreve's, for the latter may be the only unquestionable psychopathological case in the novel— in his capacity for sadism, the emphatic vicariousness of his pleasures, and so on.

vitality. He is said to speak in a "flat, curiously dead voice" (258), or in an "almost sullen flat tone" (255); he displays a "brooding bemusement" in a room that is "tomb-like." Quentin also reveals explicitly his feeling of tiredness, of repetition, and of deadness, and what is most interesting about these revelations is their contrast with his imaginative powers. This paradox, of course, has a literary precedent; it might simply be the stock schizophrenia of the seer, the man whose powers of vision are extraordinary but who is exhausted by them because he, at last, is only mortal. In Quentin's case, however, the paradox stems not from an emphasis upon his imaginative activity, but from an insistence upon his passivity: *"Yes,"* he thinks, *"I have heard too much, I have been told too much; I have had to listen to too much"* (207). This paradox of vitality and deadness, of Quentin as active seer and passive sounding board for all the voices he has ever heard, is pervasive in his narrative, and, considering our optimistic view of his perspective, this paradox is crucial.

Quentin's exhausted despair is most often associated with the voice of his father, and it is suggested in this way that Quentin's problem may be, as in the possible views of previous narrators, psychological. But this obsessive concern with his father is only significant and, perhaps, only exists for him in terms of the telling of the story:

> *Am I going to have to have to hear it all again* he thought *I am going to have to hear it all over again I am already hearing it all over again I am listening to it all over again I shall have to never listen to anything else but this again forever so apparently not only a man never outlives his father but not even his friends and acquaintances do. . . .*
> (277)

This paradox of imaginative vitality as opposed to exhaustion and deadness is aligned with another, which comes to our attention when Quentin tells Shreve that it was he, Quentin, who told his father the rest of the story on the basis of what he discovered out at Sutpen's mansion, and when he admits that at the mansion, even though he saw Clytie and Henry Sutpen, he was told nothing. Shreve says: ". . . it just came out of the terror and the fear after she turned you loose . . . and she looked at you and you saw it was not rage but terror . . . and she didn't tell you in the actual words because even in the terror she kept the secret; nevertheless she told you, or at least all of a sudden you knew—" (350–351). The case for Quentin's clairvoyance that Shreve presents here may be seen to be a substantiation of the vitality I have mentioned, and a reader may feel that Quentin really can know without being told, and see without knowing. In view of the narrators that have preceded him, however, and of our awareness of his own sense of frustration and futility, the fact that Quentin's vision springs from what is apparently nothing becomes a problem. In his discovery of Henry Sutpen at the mansion we may see an enactment of this polarity of vision and nothingness, and this dramatic moment itself, I think, takes the form of a negation of vision and of imaginative vitality. The impact of the supposed dialogue between Quentin and Henry is great, but this impact depends upon the fact that nothing is said:

And you are——?
Henry Sutpen.
And you have been here——?
Four years.
And you came home——?
To die. Yes.
To die?
Yes. To die.
And you have been here——?
Four years.
And you are——?
Henry Sutpen. (373)

This dialogue is a kind of play within a play; it is a crystallization of the sources of Quentin's vision and of the vision itself: nothing happens and nothing is said, but Quentin sees and knows. The qualities of this moment, of course, are anything but persuasive as to the reality or relevance of Quentin's imaginative perceptions. If his vision arises out of clairvoyance, this very clairvoyance has the tone of despair: in Quentin the moment of supposed perception is dramatized as a moment of hypnotic and futile circularity. This dialogue serves, rather than to demonstrate Quentin's powers as a seer, to reassert the elements of the paradox I have noted: it possesses imaginative intensity and the suggestion of meaning as opposed to its circularity and deadness, and I suggest that the sense of torturous repetition here is the same as that which Quentin feels in his despair at hearing and telling the story again and again. Here, however, we realize that this hypnotic futility lies at the foundation of Quentin's imaginative vitality; his vitality arises from deadness.

There is nothing but the talking, it seems, and the talking is dead, futile, circular. Quentin's narrative is significant not as the resolution that a reader has expected but only as the summation of all the speculation and misguided intensity that has preceded it. The anonymous narrator—whom we may associate with Faulkner—defines the Quentin–Shreve dialogue in these terms: ". . . the two of them creating between them, out of the rag-tag and bob-ends of old tales and talking, people who perhaps had never existed at all anywhere" (303). Henry Sutpen, we know, "existed," but he existed only as part of a dialogue that is for Quentin the reminder of his failure to understand what the story means, the reminder that each attempt to understand, each vision, arises out of a moment of failure. Quentin's very assertion that

he "knows" is inseparable from his conviction that he cannot know—
a conviction displayed in his sense of futile repetition, in his implied
awareness that his ability to "see" is based upon this same futility, and
in a simple, literal admission to Shreve. "Do you understand it?"
Shreve asks, and the exchange continues:

> "I dont know," Quentin said. "Yes, of course I understand it." They
> breathed in the darkness. After a moment Quentin said: "I dont know."
> "Yes. You dont know. You dont even know about the old dame, the
> Aunt Rosa."
> "Miss Rosa," Quentin said.
> "All right. You dont even know about her. . . . Do you?"
> "No," Quentin said peacefully. He could taste the dust. (362)

Quentin resembles his father and Rosa Coldfield in that his story
is founded upon what he cannot know, but he is distinguished from
them by the persistence and intensity of his attempt to make the story
meaningful. There is a distinct progression in *Absalom, Absalom!*
from the placid and remote speculation of Mr. Compson through the
narrow but more immediate incapacity of Rosa to Quentin's attempt,
and this final attempt is both more ambitious and more seriously frustrated than those of previous narrators. It is no longer a question of
Mr. Compson's errors or Rosa's ignorance: there can be no errors or
ignorance in a narrative world where we are concerned with what
cannot be meaningful or what may not exist as comprehensible experience at all.

Instead of an answer to what we had assumed was a puzzle, we
encounter in Quentin's narrative the indication that the puzzle itself
may not be real, that the gap between experience and meaning in
this novel must remain unbridgeable, and that the narrative is only,
after all, words, only a product of "old tales and talking." The paradox of Quentin's narrative is that he forms this "talking" into a vital,
articulated vision while demonstrating—and of this he is aware—that
its basis is only dead speculation upon a dead past.

The tension between imagined reality and empty words that we
find sustained in Quentin's narrative is never resolved in *Absalom,
Absalom!* It may be said to be explained, however, if we consider its
relation to the unreal story it creates, to the conception and progress
of Thomas Sutpen's "design."

"Sutpen's trouble was innocence," we are told as Quentin begins
his account. "All of a sudden he discovered, not what he wanted to do
but what he just had to do, had to do it whether he wanted to or not"
(220). Sutpen has been sent with a message to the mansion of a white
planter whom he has repeatedly watched lounging in a barrel-stave
hammock; he is thinking of the house and "thinking how at last he
was going to see the inside of it, see what else a man was bound to own

who could have a special nigger to hand him his liquor" (229). A "monkey nigger" meets him at the door, and even while he is talking, telling Sutpen never to come to the front door again, Sutpen has flashes of memory concerning his previous experience with Negroes:

> You knew that you could hit them, he told Grandfather, and they would not hit back or even resist. But you did not want to, because they (the niggers) were not it, not what you wanted to hit; that you knew when you hit them you would just be hitting a child's toy balloon with a face painted on it, a face slick and smooth and distended and about to burst into laughing, and so you did not dare strike it because it would merely burst and you would rather let it walk on out of your sight than to have stood there in the loud laughing. (230)

"The niggers" somehow prevent one's assaulting whatever it is that is important; their faces are the faces of balloons that—if one takes action against them—burst into laughter, "the roaring waves of mellow laughter meaningless and terrifying and loud" (232). Sutpen characterizes the barrier that prevents him from entering the house as something so artificial and empty as to be unassailable, a barrier that can only serve to reassert the futility of his situation.

The parallels between Sutpen and Ahab here are so striking as to be worth detailed comment. The significance of the "monkey nigger" for Sutpen is that of an artificial barrier that prevents him from penetrating to what he has assumed is a reality. Ahab would call it a "pasteboard mask"; for Sutpen it is a "balloon face." Ahab, on the one hand, is conscious of many such masks in the visual and verbal universe; they are all the suggestions, omens, and half-meanings that torture him in their uncertainty and multiplicity. Sutpen's particular problem at the moment, on the other hand, is less sophisticated and more simply a matter of deprivation. It is a social, not a natural, artificiality with which he is concerned, and this single absence of meaning—the fact that he cannot enter the house—becomes for him, as I shall try to show later, a universal negation. The color significance works almost too well here: Ahab's tortured uncertainty is incarnated in the "colorless all-color" of whiteness, whereas Sutpen's sense of complete futility and negation is symbolized in the blackness of the "monkey nigger." Both colors are generally significant as the expressions of a nothingness.

Sutpen is not yet, however, explicitly conscious of such a nothingness. He runs into the woods and attempts to understand what has happened. It was not the "nigger" that was important, he later tells General Compson:

> The nigger was just another balloon face slick and distended . . . during that instant in which, before he knew it, something in him had escaped and—he unable to close the eyes of it—was looking out from within the balloon face just as the man who did not even have to wear the shoes

he owned, whom the laughter which the balloon held barricaded and protected from such as he, looked out from whatever invisible place he (the man) happened to be at the moment, at the boy outside the barred door in his patched garments and splayed bare feet, looking through and beyond the boy, he himself seeing his own father and sisters and brothers as the owner, the rich man (not the nigger) must have been seeing them all the time—as cattle, creatures heavy and without grace, brutely evacuated into a world without hope or purpose for them, who would in turn spawn with brutish and vicious prolixity, populate, double treble and compound . . . with for sole heritage that expression on a balloon face bursting with laughter which had looked out at some unremembered and nameless progenitor who had knocked at a door when he was a little boy and had been told by a nigger to go around to the back. . . . (234–235)

What Sutpen himself appears to mean by the discovery of his "innocence" is the birth of a kind of self-consciousness; "something in him had escaped," and as the white owner has done before and does now Sutpen looks out upon himself. In terms of this view Sutpen and his descendants become purposeless animals, participants in a brutish chaos whose heritage is the balloon face and the laughter.

The boy's feelings of senselessness and futility are defined in terms of the plantation owner's position inside the big white house. He reflects that he can do nothing to reach the man, that if the house were on fire he would be unable to warn its owner:

". . . *there aint any good or harm either in the living world that I can do to him.* It was like that, he said, like an explosion—a bright glare that vanished and left nothing, no ashes nor refuse; just a limitless flat plain with the severe shape of his intact innocence rising from it like a monument; that innocence instructing him as calm as the others had ever spoken, using his own rifle analogy to do it with, and when it said *them* in place of *he* or *him,* it meant more than all the human puny mortals under the sun that might lie in hammocks all afternoon with their shoes off: He thought 'If you were fixing to combat them that had the fine rifles, the first thing you would do would be to get yourself the nearest thing to a fine rifle you could borrow or steal or make, wouldn't it?' and he said Yes." (238)

Sutpen feels a complete impotence; his significance is totally negative. The awareness of negation, which was previously suggested in blackness, now takes a spatial form. He conceives an image of himself rising from a "plain" that is flat and without limits, and his "innocence" is defined both as this image in the midst of nothingness and that which instructs him how to overcome the nothingness. He must combat "them," and "them" means more, we are told, than a group of socially defined mortals; it is not simply the class, perhaps, but the rules by which the class is established. He will combat these rules by means of the possessions that express the rules, by means of the signs and tokens of the social system, "land and niggers and a fine house" (238).

Sutpen's design is thus social in form; he is attempting to make use of the social system to overcome that system. Like Ahab, he attacks the artificial quality of his experience—which separates him from what he assumes will be a reality—and like Ahab Sutpen employs as a means of progress the artificial itself, the social structure that prevents him from entering the house. By entering the house, Sutpen will be enabled to transform himself and his descendants. They are to be "riven forever free from brutehood" and to have—like Sutpen himself—a meaningful identity (261).

This identity is finally based on the acquiring of possessions, which in accordance with the social structure will express the meaning that Sutpen desires. In Ahab's case a multiple artifice is to be penetrated and reduced to a single revelation by one final thrust of a harpoon; for Sutpen the void of his life is to be filled with possessions and descendants, which in turn must be expressive of a completely controlled and defined design. What the meaning of the design is, exactly, has not been defined as yet; Sutpen, in fact, does not seem to know what it is, but he is convinced that it will be meaning, an alleviation of his vision of chaos and impotence.

A reader's conception of the nature of Sutpen's design takes its form at the outset from what seems antithetical to the design—hollowness, arbitrariness, unreality, impotence—and this continues to be so as he proceeds through the story of Sutpen. For example, Sutpen's first wife, as we learn from the speculations of Quentin and Shreve, was part Negro; it is this that Sutpen appears to be talking about when he declares that a certain aspect of his wife and child would have made his work toward the design an "ironic delusion," and he later enlarges upon this as follows: "I was faced with condoning a fact which had been foisted upon me without my knowledge during the process of building toward my design, which meant the absolute and irrevocable negation of the design; or in holding to my original plan for the design in pursuit of which I had incurred this negation" (273).[3] This passage is characteristic of those by which Sutpen and the narrators express the design; in it there is defined a particular negation of the design, a specific and temporary failure, and the design is given shape in terms of what it is not.

It is the Negro blood in his wife and son, we may suppose, to which Sutpen objects and that constitutes this particular "negation," and it seems clear that the design is intensely social in its method. It is just the fanatical intensity of Sutpen's supposedly social aspirations, in fact, that is most problematic. Quentin remarks that Sutpen need not have

---

[3] This sentence may be best understood if we observe a grammatical parallelism that Faulkner has neglected to establish: read "or *with* holding" for "or *in* holding."

rejected his wife and child, that he might have bluffed the matter out somehow, but that he was apparently forced to reject them by his "conscience" (266). The quality of this "conscience" may be illuminated if we consider Sutpen's later refusal to recognize the same child, now Charles Bon, as his son—the refusal that ultimately results in the collapse of the entire design.

Bon's visits to the plantation, as Mr. Compson suggests to Quentin, are a metaphorical reenactment of Sutpen's childhood experience: ". . . he stood there at his own door, just as he had imagined, planned, designed, and sure enough after fifty years the forlorn nameless and homeless lost child came to knock at it and no monkey-dressed nigger anywhere under the sun to come to the door and order the child away" (267). No "monkey-dressed nigger," perhaps, because now the boy himself, Bon, contains in his Negro blood the means of his own prohibition; in this way Sutpen need not order him away; at any rate, he does not. He simply does nothing. He refuses to take the only action that would alleviate the problem and enable him to continue with his design; he refuses to recognize Bon on any terms. It is as if his childhood imaginings have come true: a boy comes to tell a man that his house is on fire and cannot be heard.[4]

Sutpen has declared to General Compson, we are told, that he felt he had made a mistake somewhere and that his inaction toward Bon— "the fact that for a time he did nothing and so perhaps helped to bring about the very situation which he dreaded"—was "not the result of any failing of courage or shrewdness or ruthlessness, but . . . the result of his conviction that it had all come from a mistake and until he discovered what that mistake had been he did not intend to risk making another one" (268). The language of this passage is mild considering the duration and the intensity of Sutpen's paralysis; his refusal to recognize Bon in any way seems insane, out of all proportion to what we suppose are the facts, and out of proportion even to the sustained bemusement that Sutpen is said to have admitted. The "choice" that he felt he had to make, as we learn later, was no choice at all; either way his design would have been destroyed. But in his choice he made no provision for direct action toward Bon, but only for either playing his "last trump card"—telling Henry that Bon is part Negro—or doing nothing.

---

[4] The phenomenon of impotence is thus dramatized also in the hypothetical account of Bon, a search for design in itself. Richard Poirier has remarked that "incest with Judith or death at the hands of his brother become the only ways in which Bon can identify himself as Sutpen's son." "Strange Gods in Jefferson, Mississippi," in *William Faulkner: Two Decades of Criticism*, ed. Frederick J. Hoffman and Olga W. Vickery (East Lansing: Michigan State College Press, 1951), p. 239. [See this volume, p. 28. Ed.] For explicit images, in Shreve's account, of Bon's failure to "penetrate" and his encounters with "nothingness," see in *Absalom, Absalom!*, for example, pp. 320, 327, 348.

What is truly inexplicable here is that Bon seems to pose no literal threat whatever to the design; if exposed as a fractionally Negro son he could not participate in the design or even oppose it, and Sutpen might have known this as well as Bon. If the only important consideration were social, also, Sutpen could have either accepted Bon and concealed his Negro blood or refused to accept him and proclaimed it. In either case a merely social design would have been unimpaired. Because Bon is surely not an insurmountable obstacle to the design in social terms, the failure to recognize him becomes significant evidence that Sutpen's demands are more than social, that if he is making use of the particular ingredients of the social system to accomplish his design, the design itself is to be defined not in terms of that system but of something more. It is more, in short, than the sum of its apparent parts.

Sutpen's frantic inaction toward Bon reveals the two important qualities of his design: that it is both an attempt to dominate the arbitrariness that Sutpen perceives in his universe and an attempt to make real the artificial significances that this arbitrariness creates. Sutpen, perhaps, sees Bon as an incarnation of both the arbitrary and the artificial, as the reincarnation, in fact, of the "monkey nigger" of his childhood and all that that figure represented. We must remember, in this connection, that before his experience at the door of the plantation house Sutpen did not question the chaos of "luck" in which he lived; it was only after that experience that this chaos became significant in terms of the meaning, or lack of meaning, of his life. In that moment at the door, Sutpen begins to demand meaning of his experience; he begins to view his world metaphorically. It is just this metaphorical vision, as I have suggested, that is most apparent when he confronts Charles Bon: Bon's Negro blood is literally insignificant, but for Sutpen it implies a crucial lack of control over past and present; in his metaphorical view it represents the total negation that he experienced at the door of the plantation house, where he first became conscious of a possible world of meaning that was beyond him. The characteristic irony of Sutpen's situation is that his demands for meaning, his fierce attempts to create a metaphor from the arbitrariness of his experience, are frustrated even in their conception; when viewed metaphorically this experience yields only what a reader may see as images that imply the unreality of metaphor—a limitless plain, a blackness, a paralysis.

The relentlessness of Sutpen's insistence upon clarity and control in his experience is constantly revealed in his treatment of what a reader might have assumed to be only literal details. He is not content with merely owning slaves, for which the social system provides, but must on numerous occasions strip to the waist and engage a Negro in savage, hand-to-hand combat, fighting until the Negro can fight no longer. This apparently insane desire to dominate his slaves again dramatizes the connection in Sutpen's mind between literal control over the elements of the system he employs and the metaphorical vision of blackness—of unreal significance and negation of self—that he possesses. By defeating the Negro, Sutpen is not only destroying a social artificiality in the relation of the parts of his design to himself but also destroying what he sees metaphorically to be the continued existence of that negation which his design was to overcome.

His will to dominate, of course, is not always displayed in such direct association to the specific metaphor of blackness, but it is always an indication of his desire for unambiguous meaning. We may consider, for example, his treatment of the French architect who designs his plantation house. He does not simply employ the architect, but possesses him completely until the house is finished. The set of conventions which the architect represents are thus redefined as Sutpen's own conventions—not arbitrary significances from a world outside Sutpen, but a part of his very being.

It should be apparent, then, that to Sutpen's mind the complete possession and control of the previously uncontrolled details of experience must inevitably result in the creation of a meaningful identity, that the clarity which is to follow from this control will be an alleviation of disorder and meaninglessness. The physical and literal order of his design are in this way an imaginative order, and his entire progress toward a moment when all the details will fall into place is an uncompromising imaginative act.

Throughout his life the desire for unambiguous order dominates Sutpen's imagination; at every crucial moment in his progress toward failure he views the details of his world as the ingredients of a metaphorical structure that he believes he can and must create. In a conversation with General Compson, he reveals the most important elements of such a metaphor; he reduces his design to what are for him its most important terms: "You see, all I wanted was just a son. Which seems to me, when I look at my contemporary scene, no exorbitant gift from nature or circumstance to demand—" (292). The very simplicity of this statement renders it incomprehensible as a literal remark, for Sutpen had two sons—two sons whose literal destruction was brought about by his demands for control and meaning, by his metaphorical view in which Charles Bon was the negation of such control.

Sutpen's conception of fatherhood, as his conception of the entire world, is founded upon the conviction that the begetting of a son is not a physical or a literal act, but an imaginative and metaphorical achievement; fatherhood is the creation of the essential element in a design, in a structure that will endure. His only desire in the years of his decline is to beget the evidence of his significance, and by doing so to complete the arrangement that he feels is not yet right; the result is the proposal that outrages Rosa Coldfield and which Quentin's father calls another "failing" of Sutpen's shrewdness. A reader, however, may wonder what else at this point Sutpen could have done, given his assumption that his mistake must lie in the arrangement and details of his design. He was a master of detail, but his mastery only resulted in failure. The futile circularity of his course is crystallized in his attempt to father a son upon Milly Jones, whose situation is reminiscent of Sutpen's own childhood, and whose grandfather bears the same relation to the balloon faces and the laughter of Negroes as did Sutpen himself as a child, but who endures it by means of the delusion that he is Sutpen. To Wash Jones "this world where he walked always in mocking and jeering echoes of nigger laughter, was just a dream and an illusion and . . . the actual world was the one where his own lonely apotheosis (Father said) galloped on the black thoroughbred" (282). Sutpen's desire for a son, in this way, brings him back to his origins, back to the brutish senselessness and lack of significance that the laugher first made apparent and that were to become the motivation of his design. Wash Jones views Sutpen as his (Jones's) apotheosis and later destroys him and it, just as Sutpen himself—in his final equivalence to Wash—has returned to his sources and thereby destroyed the apotheosis of himself that was half-created but could not endure: that apotheosis by which he was both the creator of meaning and the product of his creation, the meaning itself, all opposed to the senseless and absurd condition where at last he ends as he began.

General Compson's remarks often support the view of the "apotheosis" that I am suggesting. He declares that Sutpen's failure must be defined in terms of a tension between sense and senselessness, between a "code" and a "maelstrom of unpredictable and unreasoning human beings" (275). And at moments he indicates that it is a matter of even greater proportions, as in Quentin's secondhand account of Sutpen's overseeing of the West Indian plantation:

> And he overseeing it, riding peacefully about on his horse while he learned the language (that meager and fragile thread, Grandfather said, by which the little surface corners and edges of men's secret and solitary lives may be joined for an instant now and then before sinking back into the darkness where the spirit cried for the first time and was not heard and will cry for the last time and will not be heard then either), not knowing that what he rode upon was a volcano, hearing the air tremble and throb at night with the drums and the chanting and not knowing that it was the heart of the earth itself he heard, who believed (Grandfather said) that earth was kind and gentle and that darkness was merely something you saw, or could not see in. . . . (251)

Here General Compson has constructed a metaphor by which the incomprehensibilities and confusions of human experience are not particular or momentary difficulties to be resolved by better language, but the expressions of a failure that is absolute and inevitable. The metaphor is that of a "darkness," a darkness that is not "merely something you saw, or could not see in."

But while Quentin's grandfather appears to suggest that the only metaphor that can be created is a vague expression of unavoidable defeat, Sutpen's glimpses of the supposed nothingness only goad him to more violent attempts to overcome it. He cannot understand the perpetuation of his impotence; he assumes again and again that he has made a mistake in the details of his design. We are told that Sutpen never loses his innocence, and this innocence may be finally defined as his conviction that the world consists of potential metaphors that need only be accumulated and arranged in order to be real.

And yet the essential quality and paradox of Sutpen's metaphorical vision of the world, again, is that by means of this vision he perceives nothing but the contradictions of it. His determination to establish order, as I have suggested, springs not only from a perception of disorder but also from a vision in which disorder becomes a void, a nothingness. His imagination, in this way, is constantly at war with itself; his attempt to overcome a lack of control, to accumulate and arrange the details of his design, is always at odds with his feeling that this lack of control is evidence of a complete absence of identity, an absolute negation of the "self" that he is striving to create. Sutpen may thus be seen both to deny and to accept General Compson's awareness of a universal "darkness." In Charles Bon, for example, he sees both a simple, literal "mistake" that might be rectified and an absolute, metaphorical contradiction of his ability to create a meaning that, while he cannot admit it as a complete negation of his efforts, paralyzes him, prevents him from acting upon the "mistake." When we consider General Compson's attitude, we may understand why Sutpen's innocence was associated with nothingness in the very conception of his design, for this innocence is what persuades Sutpen throughout his career that meaning can and must be created from disorder even while he appears to view this same disorder as the evidence of absolute negation.

The course of his design is not simply circular; it is no course at all. His conviction that the world consists of potential metaphor that only needs arranging—the conviction that is the guiding principle of this design and of all design—is inseparable from his sense of perfect futility. His maniacal desire to dominate his world is thus explained, for even a momentary failure becomes the metaphorical expression of the void in which he somehow believes and yet which he cannot accept. His attempt to make his world a metaphor succeeds only in reasserting that the only possible metaphor is that of "darkness."

Sutpen's design thus contains its own destruction, and his course of action and vision is inevitably a series of failures. The particular failures of Sutpen, however, may seem unsatisfactory to a reader as evi-

dence for a more general failure. It is possible to reject General Compson's conviction that all is a darkness, in terms of which, as I have
tried to show, the interdependence in Sutpen's design between the
desire for meaning and the feeling of ultimate failure is revealed.

The question that arises is whether such a connection between not
only order and disorder but also meaning and darkness is necessary
throughout the world of this novel, for in Sutpen's case it seems suspect in two ways. The vision of meaninglessness from which the design
arises and which it implies throughout in the manner of its failures
may be questioned if we consider Sutpen's naïveté—the naïveté of a
boy born in the mountains of west Virginia and possessing perhaps
the simplest code of logic and morality. If, when this code is destroyed,
he becomes aware of the complete absence of meaning, it is possible
to say that this awareness is simply a product of the narrowness of his
mind. In the same manner, both the intensity and the failure of the
man's struggle toward his design, depending as they do upon the initial
vision, may be seen as a mania arising from the outrage of a peculiarly
rigid imagination. In short, the childhood vision was just what half of
Sutpen's mind thought it was: only a temporary confusion that could
be, with the right method, alleviated. The second objection, then, is
that Sutpen does not use the right method, that there is something
wrong with the particular metaphor that he is trying to create. Because the implements of his design are those of the social structure of
the South, and because he wields these implements with even more
ruthless energy than they permit in the first place, we might conclude
that Sutpen is simply an immoral man in a moral book, and that
therefore he must fail.

It may be noted that here Sutpen is again the counterpart of Ahab,
for we have seen that the latter figure can be viewed in just these
terms: as a monomaniac whose limitations are those of insanity and
folly or as a being of heroic stature who may be termed insane only
because he attempts to move beyond the fatal limits of the world. And
to view Sutpen as immoral or even insane, of course, is to reduce his
significance drastically. In its relation to the narrative method of
Quentin, however, and to the paradox of vitality and deadness that I
have mentioned, the history of Sutpen's design becomes meaningful,
as I shall now show more clearly, as one expression of the fallibility of
all order and all imagination in *Absalom, Absalom!* If Sutpen's problem may be termed a kind of imaginative schizophrenia, his particular
insanity is general throughout the entire novel.

I have previously dwelt at length upon Quentin's failure to understand the story he articulates, but it is necessary at this point to examine a few details of this failure in order to show that it correlates
with Sutpen's history so as to illuminate the structural theme of the

novel. When Quentin admits his lack of comprehension to Shreve, for
example, he does so "peacefully," and at that moment he can taste the
"dust." The "dust" is the dust rising around the buggy as he and
Rosa Coldfield make their nocturnal journey to Sutpen's Hundred:

> . . . the dust cloud moving on, enclosing them with not threat exactly
> but maybe warning, bland, almost friendly, warning, as if to say, *Come
> on if you like. But I will get there first; accumulating ahead of you I will
> arrive first, lifting, sloping gently upward under hooves and wheels so
> that you will find no destination but will merely abrupt gently onto a
> plateau and a panorama of harmless and inscrutable night and there
> will be nothing for you to do but return.* . . . (175)

The dust is suggestive not only of mortality but also of chaos; it is the
precursor of a "plateau" that resembles the flat plain of meaninglessness in Sutpen's childhood vision; it implies that when Quentin arrives he will discover *"nothing."* [5] And although Henry Sutpen is there
at the mansion, Quentin learns nothing from him. His supposed actual
conversation with Henry demonstrates that there is indeed nothing to
do but return. In this way the flashes of perception that Quentin displays are implied to be parallel to Sutpen's design in that both arise
from a precognition of meaninglessness and from a subsequent, anticlimactic awareness of a flat and barren nothingness.

Another parallel to Sutpen arises when the anonymous narrator
describes the room at Harvard as "this snug monastic coign, this
dreamy and heatless alcove of what we call the best of thought." The
room is the point of most advantage, where the history of the Sutpens
will certainly be understood if it can be. The narrator continues by
remarking that Mr. Compson's letter has filled the room with "unratiocinative djinns and demons" (258). The room is filled, perhaps,
with the ghostly presences of the Sutpens, who are "unratiocinative"
in some supposed lack of systematic thought. Somewhat later the matter
becomes clearer: "in the cold room . . . dedicated to that best of
ratiocination which after all was a good deal like Sutpen's morality
and Miss Coldfield's demonizing . . ." (280). An explicit equivalence
is drawn here between the logic of Sutpen that failed and the logic of
Quentin and Shreve as they attempt to comprehend the failure; they
indulge in the "best of thought" and are able only to demonstrate
their own similarity to Sutpen and to the narrators that have preceded
them.

Earlier Quentin visualizes the death of Thomas Sutpen in a way
that further supports the schematic organization for the novel that I
am proposing: ". . . *she heard the whip too though not the scythe,
no whistling air, no blow, nothing since always that which merely con-*

---

[5] The connection between mortality and disorder in the imagination of Quentin
and Faulkner himself becomes most obvious in *The Sound and the Fury*, which I
shall consider later. [See Guetti, op. cit., pp. 148–53. Ed.]

summates punishment evokes a cry while that which evokes the last silence occurs in silence" (185). Sutpen's death evokes "the last silence," and that silence is the entire narrative of *Absalom, Absalom!* All of the particular uncertainties, inadequacies, and cruxes of this narrative, although they may appear to be of only temporary significance initially, are shown to have a larger relevance; they are all part of a general and absolute inability to render experience meaningful—an inability that the supposed story of Sutpen itself implies.

Sutpen's problem, then, becomes part of a larger, thematic problem. And it must be added here that unlike Quentin's father and Rosa, whose information is incomplete, Sutpen is a master of detail; he accumulates all the literal facts necessary to his design. In his own terms, of course, he is sure that he has made a mistake in detail, but, again, his mistake is shown to be of greater dimensions than this—a mistake of vision itself, that "innocent" vision which dictates that the world is metaphor and must mean something, and in terms of which a disorder becomes a "darkness."

This is the vision to which every narrator in the novel holds in his account of Sutpen. Mr. Compson's attitude that the story does not explain is understandable considering his lack of "information"; his mistake lies in the fact that he sees this inexplicability as a metaphor. The inconsistency of details, for him, is an expression of a great meaning that has to do with fate. Rosa, too, possesses a view of the would as metaphor. Her inability to understand Sutpen and the events surrounding him is significant to her as an expression of Sutpen's demonhood. She seems superior to Quentin's father, however, in the intensity with which she asserts the unreality of the experience upon which the story is founded and in the apparently greater cost of her frustrated attempts to give it meaning. She may be said to question her own metaphors more thoroughly.

In Quentin's case the matter of the story appears to become more consistent; of the narrators of the book he is most analogous to Sutpen in that he too is capable in the accumulation of details, details that should comprise a pattern that will be controlled and significant. Nonetheless he cannot understand, cannot achieve the meaning that both he and Shreve think exists. His inability is partly expressed, again, in his sources, in the approximations that he inherits from Rosa and from his father and grandfather as well as in his perceptions that seem to arise from nothing. His most crucial moment of vision takes place in the dialogue, which is so hypnotically repetitive, with Henry Sutpen. This dialogue indicates that what I have called "approximations" and "nothing" are really in Quentin's case the same thing and the same source. We have been prepared for it as a climactic moment of understanding and as such it is a failure. And it is a failure that repeats itself, the repetition suggesting that it means something, that it is a metaphor, and the same repetition denying that the metaphor can be realized. In this way it is equivalent to all the stories that Quentin has heard since he was old enough to listen, stories repeated over and over, whose unfulfilled reiteration both asserts their metaphorical nature and denies it.

It is this tension between the meaningful and the meaningless that Quentin has inherited in the approximations of his father, and it is understandable that he feels he must escape from his father and hence from the unrealized story itself. His only moment of peace in the novel comes when for a moment he dissolves the tension, relinquishes the need for meaning that was bequeathed to him as a history of uncertainties, and admits to Shreve "peacefully" that he does not understand.[6]

In a remark that is relevant to the idea of the "last silence," the anonymous narrator speaks of Sutpen as "Quentin's Mississippi shade who in life had acted and reacted to the minimum of logic and morality, who dying had escaped it completely, who dead remained not only indifferent but impervious to it, somehow a thousand times more potent and alive" (280). Sutpen is more "alive" because he is impervious to attempts to understand him. The meanings that surround him lend him a vitality that arises out of their impotence and deadness. The analogy with the supposed story of Sutpen himself is clear, for in that story his presence and power depended upon impotence not simply in the motivation but in the definition of the design, for the design as an attempted metaphorical vision is articulated in what it cannot do, in the intensity and scope of its failures. Thomas Sutpen's power is inseparable from his impotence, and it is in understanding this paradox that we may better understand the tension of vitality and deadness in Quentin and all the narrative uncertainties of the "last silence."

Quentin's vision, like Sutpen's, is composed of an intense desire to perceive and the conviction that his perception must fail. His situation is as tortured as Sutpen's because his inheritance is a body of approximations that possess contradictory implications: first, that they are evidence of the progress toward meaning; second, that the very fact that there are only approximations, repeated and sustained, denies the possibility of achieving a meaning.

The mode of expression to which Quentin is heir is incredibly powerful; a reader feels that something is always just about to be defined, the heart of the problem revealed. The story which Quentin tells, furthermore, possesses all the more imaginative vitality *because* it is never composed; it is surrounded with countless possible significances;

---

[6] Our knowledge, from *The Sound and the Fury*, that Quentin commits suicide in the spring of this year is surely relevant here, and would suggest a final relinquishment and "dissolution of the tension."

the multiple suggestions by which the story becomes so powerful continue to exist precisely because no single meaning is ever achieved. The vitality of the entire narrative of *Absalom, Absalom!* depends upon the inability to create a single, dominant metaphor; the multiple significances arise out of a permanent stalemate, a failure, a deadness. It is in this way that Thomas Sutpen is most alive because he is dead and that the language of the entire novel is most suggestive of meaning because it constitutes the refutation of a dominant meaning.

As I have attempted to show, it is impossible for Quentin to move beyond a language that is approximate. In his very moments of perception the significances he remarks seem to spring from a denial of meaning and to be given their suggestiveness by the denial, whether it takes the form of the multiple, qualified speculations of all the narrators who have preceded him or that of a hypnotically repeated dialogue that never comes to issue. Quentin's, and a reader's, position regarding the story he tells is always one of uncertainty, where a meaning seems to exist and not to exist. It is ultimately characterized in the relation that Quentin imagines between the men who have come to take Henry Sutpen and Jim Bond, the part Negro idiot who is the last element of the Sutpen story: "They could hear him; he didn't seem to ever get any further away but they couldn't get any nearer and maybe in time they could not even locate the direction any more of the howling" (376). Bond represents the entire story: he is potential meaning, always just out of reach, but asserting in his idiot howling the negation of meaning. The suggestiveness of his presence is denied by the very quality that establishes it, his incomprehensibility. Shreve, with characteristic callousness, reminds Quentin: ". . . you've got him there still. You still hear him at night sometimes. Don't you?" (378) But a reader is aware that no reminder is necessary, that Bond represents the constant tension that haunts Quentin, the story that must be meaningful and cannot be. For Sutpen, Bond would have been the final symbol of nothingness, the last failure, and he thus embodies the defeat of both narrator and character. He is General Compson's "spirit" crying in the "darkness," and he is a refutation of all that "design," for both Quentin and Sutpen, ever meant.

In my discussions of *Moby-Dick* and "Heart of Darkness," I have frequently remarked Ishmael's and Marlow's reliance upon approximate language of various kinds, from obviously limited special and artificial vocabularies to intensely qualified and just as intensely rendered allusions, reports, and figures. It should be clear now that Quentin Compson, like Marlow, is Ishmael's counterpart in his use of verbal approximations—specifically both in his use of narrative matter taken or inherited from sources outside himself and in his own characteristic imaginative tensions of the artificial and the real,

deadness and vitality. It should be clear also that the "last silence" of
Absalom, Absalom! is equivalent to the "dumb blankness, full of
meaning" of *Moby-Dick*. In each case profundity is expressed by the
fact that the attempt to achieve profundity must always be qualified,
that all the suggestive voices must always be "silent." I have characterized this use of language generally as "simile," in its opposition to
the potentially metaphorical visions of Ahab, Kurtz, and Sutpen, and
I shall now summarize particularly how the narrative of *Absalom, Absalom!* exhibits its quality as extended simile.

Although the quality of this narrative as simile is most obvious
when it is laced with words and phrases like "as though," "perhaps,"
"I think," and "I would like to believe," and most emphatic when
Quentin demonstrates the suggestive failure that all these tags imply,
this quality is shown to be a constant property of the entire narrative
in that Quentin is the sum of all the narrators and in that the anonymous narrator—in a striking extension of Ishmael's unwillingness to
commit himself—refuses to sanction the entire narrative as anything
more than hypothesis. The story thus becomes one great "as though"
based upon a supposed body of literal details like those of the "Chronology" and "Genealogy" and the attempt to make these details meaningful. All of the narrators attempt to compose these details into a
story by which they will become significant both to narrator and
listener, and the result is always a suspect relation between literal and
metaphorical represented in the approximated story—an extended
simile whose assertion of potential meaning insists that such meaning
must only be potential. In this way the inability of the imagination to
proceed beyond approximation is reflected in both the theme and
the method of *Absalom, Absalom!,* and this phenomenon constitutes,
I think, the success and the failure of this novel.

In Sutpen's conviction that order lies just beyond his reach and in
the constant frustration of his attempts to grasp it, he is himself—like
Ahab at the last—a kind of living simile. He represents a distinct kind
of language that in his failure is shown to be inadequate. And in his
case the simile into which he is transformed is demonstrated to be
both the beginning and the end of metaphor, both a step forward to
and backward from metaphor. We feel justified in describing him in
this way because, as I have suggested previously, both a meaning that
he desires and his own sense of its negation are observable in the
source and progress of his design. Sutpen's particular negation, furthermore, may be seen to partake of the "darkness" that General Compson
holds to be universal and inevitable.

For the narrators of the novel, however, "darkness" is apparent only
by reference to the hypothetical story of Sutpen. We are unable, for
this reason, to say just why it is that Quentin fails to make the story
more than hypothesis. In the case of Sutpen, again, we are presented

with a defined and dramatic polarity: "design" and "darkness." His history and his ultimate defeat may be understood in terms of a conflict between these elements. For Quentin there is no such conflict, but only what might be the result of one; the particular vitality-deadness paradox exhibited in his perceptions may well be simply an inherited quality of imagination. Even though his attempt to understand the story is unquestionably genuine, and even though his failure often seems generally persuasive, he may be said to be restricted by his inheritance from previous speakers of both an unresolved story and the conviction that it must remain unresolved. And if we return to these speakers, we find that even here there is no conclusive or even dramatic conflict which decides that the imagination must inevitably fail. The failures of Rosa Coldfield, Quentin's father, and thus of Quentin himself seem at worst a matter of psychology and at best a matter of circumstance, of limitations acting upon them from without and for which they seem not responsible, limitations imposed, of course, by Faulkner. In either case their defeat appears unconvincing as an instance of a defeat to which all men are liable, or as evidence of a "darkness."

The ambiguous problem that the narrators reveal may become generally meaningful, again, in relation to the conflict in Sutpen, but this conflict is not only open to various specific qualifications but also is itself the general product of the narrators' speculations, and we have come full circle. If the inconclusiveness of the narrative is the result of a conflict like the hypothetical struggle of Thomas Sutpen, that conflict does not appear in the narrative except as a creation of and an example of the inconclusiveness itself. The "darkness" itself is only a possibility, and the presentation of imaginative failure as a theme has its ultimate source not in a real tension that is brought to issue in the novel but in the anonymous narrator's declaration that the story may not exist at all. The failure to define a story and to create a metaphor, in other words, seems assumed and lacks force as evidence of the necessity of failure.

For Faulkner, then, the use of extended simile and the defeat it implies becomes the total narrative method: not a dramatized struggle with whatever may lie beyond imagination, and not simply a structural theme that he assumes, but a manner of proceeding that implies that as a theme it is unstable. The fact that the supposed conflict between design and darkness is itself unrealizable may be seen to be an extension of this theme when we consider that Faulkner postulates the failure of *all* metaphor.

This failure was exhibited at the outset in the narratives of Quentin's father and Rosa Coldfield, for the fallibility of both these speakers was expressed in their attempt to transform kinds of disorder, their own inabilities to understand, into metaphor. For Mr. Compson this disorder meant "Fate"; for Rosa it meant Sutpen's "demonhood." In either version the characters of the Sutpen story were shown in futile conflict with something supernatural—in Mr. Compson's case a supernatural force and in Rosa's a supernatural entity. The distinction between these narrators and General Compson, of course, rests in the fact that Quentin's grandfather will postulate only the metaphor of "darkness," but this distinction is not so meaningful as one might suppose, for the "darkness" too suggests the presence of supernatural powers who cannot be defeated. The imaginative failure here thus becomes a metaphor itself, an assertion of the order of the universe, in terms of which Sutpen's defeat is explainable and significant.

This matter may be clarified if we remember that in *Moby-Dick* the ineffable is supposed to have, at least until Ahab finally fails, a metaphorical existence in the white whale and that Melville suggests, in this manner, the reality of a conflict between mind and the ineffable. In "Heart of Darkness," too, we are still dealing—because of Marlow's persistent moral concern—with the "powers of darkness," even though such powers lose significance throughout and the polarity between mind and darkness is, I think, finally destroyed. In both cases the attempts at order are suggested to be meaningful—again, in different degrees—in terms of their conflict with the nature of the universe, with the ineffable.

In *Absalom, Absalom!* the darkness itself—and the metaphorical struggle—is hypothetical. We are thus allowed to question Sutpen's vision of design and nothingness—the vision that causes his failure— and we may even see it as an example of a kind of schizophrenia. In the case of Quentin Compson, where "darkness" is not even directly suggested, the temptation to use the language of psychopathology is even greater, and we cannot understand why he appears to be the most sympathetically treated narrator. The paradox here is that Quentin seems most psychologically deranged precisely because in terms of the theme of the novel he is most sane: he does not worship the fictions of fate or darkness, but simply, and desperately, confesses that he does not understand. Faulkner suggests in this way that the failure here is just that; it cannot be alleviated or explained by any metaphor, even a metaphor of inevitable failure. In other words, this failure can be displayed conscientiously and realistically only be exhibiting a flat absence of imaginative control and the terrible cost of that absence.

It is for this reason, I think, that Faulkner deliberately places the story beyond his narrators; the essential imaginative problem, he appears to suggest, can be consistently demonstrated only in the failure to create any story at all. No dramatic tensions or conflicts may exist unequivocally in this novel, and we are left with the sheer verbal disorder that reflects the inability to create a fictional world. But the failure to compose a story is the failure to compose a novel, and we have only Faulkner's word that the failure was the unavoidable result of his most conscientious perception, his word for the necessity of defeat.

The last paradox of *Absalom, Absalom!*, then, is the complete interdependence of success with failure in the novel, and this paradox cannot be resolved. That the imagination must fail is not really demonstrated in the novel, and the lack of imaginative control in the novel is, on the one hand, Faulkner's insufficiency. On the other hand, the novel suggests that such a failure could not be demonstrated; it suggests that to resolve the matter by creating a "darkness" is to falsify. This novel is the most thoroughgoing of those works of fiction that call into question the possibilities of language and meaning; as an immense display of fallen language and as a revelation of the nature of this language, it seems unparalleled. In it Faulkner insists that, as Sutpen's active force and Quentin's imaginative vitality arise from and are exhibited in their failure, the greatest success of language itself is to create a potential of meaning that must remain unrealized, a tension between order and disorder that cannot be resolved but only repeated, and repeated. Language may be defined in this way, however, only because no meaning is ever achieved, because no metaphor is ever constructed.

It is not simply that *Absalom, Absalom!* is possibly one kind of novel or another but that it is possibly no novel at all. Faulkner's insistence that the imagination must fail completely can never be evaluated because it can only remain an insistence. The supposed struggle that it implies could only be revealed metaphorically and thus cannot be revealed—given the insistence—at all. Faulkner's position is superficially equivalent to that of Rosa Coldfield herself, when Rosa questions the metaphors she employs; his assertion that the function of language can only be to create a hypothetical and insoluble potential is *"that true wisdom which can comprehend that there is a might-have-been which is more true than truth"* (143). It may be that Faulkner's inability to dramatize this wisdom, as he suggests, is indicative of a general and inevitable failure of the human mind to order and of his imaginative balance in dealing with this failure; it may be also that, like Rosa, he is not balanced at all, that he is simply unable to allow this wisdom to be tested. There is no way of knowing.

Appendix A:
An Index to *Absalom, Absalom!*

by Thomas E. Connolly

The following skeletal outline of *Absalom, Absalom!* may help to unravel this complex novel for the undergraduate reader and it may help the teacher in preparing the text for presentation. Faulkner's manipulation of time and point of view, for instance, become more obvious in such an outline. Page references, which appear in parentheses, are to the Modern Library edition of the novel.

The Characters of Absalom, Absalom!

Quentin (7) Compson (9) [III]: The principal narrator; aged 20, in 1909 (10); born 1891; died 1910 (383).

Shreve (173) [Shrevlin McCannon (383)]: Roommate of Quentin Compson at Harvard (173); born in Edmonton (385), Alberta (258) [in 1890 (383); attended Harvard from 1909 to 1914].

[Jason Richmond] Compson (11): Quentin's father; narrates parts of the novel.

Colonel (126) Thomas Sutpen (9): Born west Virginia in 1807; one of 7 children; poor white, Scotch-English (381); arrives in Jefferson one Sunday in June 1833 (11); aged 25 in 1833 (17); marries Ellen Coldfield; he is a debased man who stages fights between his wild Negroes for entertainment; even fights them himself; forces his son Henry to watch; Henry gets sick at sight, but his sister Judith watches secretly and voluntarily (29–30); expert pistol shot (33); acquires 100 square miles from Chickasaw Indians; uses his last coin (a Spanish coin) to record deed (34); returns two months later with a captive French architect and 20 slaves (35, 37); borrows his first seed cotton from General Compson to start plantation (40–41); first goes to church

"An Index to Absalom, Absalom!" *(Editor's title) by Thomas E. Connolly. From* College English 25 *(November, 1963): 110–14. Copyright © 1963 by the National Council of Teachers of English. Reprinted by permission of the publisher and Thomas E. Connolly.*

in 1838 where he sees Ellen (41); he got his land from Ikkemotubbe
(44); after his deliberate siege of Mr. Coldfield and Ellen, he disappears
again and returns in 2 months with a fabulous cargo of rugs, mahogany, crystal, etc. to furnish his house (43–44); is engaged to Ellen
(1838); is arrested on suspicion about furniture (47); is married in
June 1838, two months after arrest (48); refuse is thrown at couple
when they leave church (56); returns home from war in 1866 (62); in
1858, he is "biggest single landowner and cotton-planter in the county"
(72); begins war as second in command to Colonel Sartoris in 1861
(80); nearing 55 in 1861 (80); visits New Orleans to learn of Bon's
association with nonwhite mistress (92–93); he decides to prevent the
marriage to Judith (93); [from p. 92 to p. 104 ff. there is constant hint-
ing that what Sutpen discovered was the mistress, not that Charles
Bon was his own son;] elected Colonel when Colonel Sartoris is deposed by his own officers (126); during war his wife dies (188); returns
from war January 1866 (158); is engaged to Rosa Coldfield 3 months
later (158); Sutpen 59 in 1866 (160); determines to restore the place
(160); is killed by Wash Jones (171–72; 284 ff.), in 1869 (181–82, 185)
because he seduced Jones's 15-year-old granddaughter and then scorned
her when she bore a girl (183, 185). [There is a discrepancy in date on
p. 185; Judith is said to be 30 when he died; thus the date of his death
would appear to be 1871 here.] Sutpen dies on August 12, 1869 (188);
he had been born in 1807 in West Virginia; his early life is narrated
(220–38); he went to West Indies to start his fortune (238); put his first
wife aside because she did not fit his design (241); got Spanish coin in
West Indies (238); the wife he repudiated was West Indian French
[Charles Bon's mother] (248); he also repudiated their child (262); he
saw Charles Bon during the war and knew he intended to marry
Judith; he confronted Henry with this fact; finally he told Henry
that Charles had Negro blood (354–55); this fact, not incest, convinced
Henry to kill Bon (355).

Eulalia Bon Sutpen: Born Haiti (381); first wife of Thomas Sutpen
(241); marries him in 1827; is divorced in 1831 (381); West Indian
French (248); father French; mother Spanish (252); she is the mother
of Charles Bon (256); she is repudiated because of her Negro blood
(266); dies in New Orleans, date unknown (381).

Henry (18) Sutpen (9): Born 1839, died 1910 (383); son of Thomas
and Ellen Sutpen (9); kills his sister's sweetheart on her wedding day
(18); 2 years older than Judith and 6 years older than Rosa Coldfield
[therefore born c. 1839] (21); 26 years old in 1864 (59); enters University
c. 1857 (70); vanishes Christmas [c. 1860] after a quarrel with his father
whom he formally abjures; renounces his birthright and rides off with
Charles Bon (78 ff.); enlists as a private (87); scarcely 20 when he
repudiates his father (91); argument with father takes place on Decem-

ber 24, 1860 (105); rescues Bon in battle when Bon is wounded (124); kills Charles Bon before his father's house for the implied reason that, though he will marry Judith, he will not renounce his mistress (132–33); drops the body at his sister's feet and vanishes again (Chapter IV); returns to Sutpen's Hundred c. 1905 (351); he meets his father on the field (353) true reason given—he decides to kill Bon when his father tells him that Bon has Negro blood (355).

Judith (15) Sutpen (9): Daughter of Ellen and Thomas Sutpen (9); niece to (15) Rosa (18), but four years older than her aunt (15); born in 1841 (59); she has inherited her father's love of evil; urges the wild Negro to drive madly (25); is engaged at 17 [c. 1858] (70); buries Charles Bon beside her mother (104); nurses the wounded during the war while waiting for news of Henry and Bon (126); for no apparent reason, she gives the only letter she received from Bon during the war to Quentin's grandmother (127–28); after much obliqueness, the letter, written in 1865, makes a direct proposal of marriage (129–32); she and Clytie make her wedding gown of scraps (132); she is 30 [see above] when her father is killed; she sells the store in 1870 (191); tells C. E. St.-V. Bon to call her "Aunt Judith" as a hint of Charles Bon's real parentage (208); nurses C. E. St.-V Bon in yellow fever; contracts disease and dies; born October 3, 1841, died February 12, 1884 (210–11).

Ellen Coldfield Sutpen (9): Born in Tennessee in 1818 [but see p. 188] (381): 2nd wife of Thomas Sutpen, sister of Miss Rosa; married in 1838 (48); in her late thirties 20 years after her marriage in 1858 (68–69); loses her reason about 1852 (69–70); born October 9, 1817, died January 23, 1863 (188).

Miss Rosa (9) Coldfield (7): About 60 at the start of the narrative in 1909 (10–11); has worn black since Appomattox in April 1865 (7); refuses to marry Sutpen (13); four years younger than her niece Judith (15); agrees to marry Sutpen (18) at the age of 20 in 1865 (19, 59); born in 1845 (59); hates her father because of her mother's death at her birth (60); starts to write poetry for the Southern Cause in the first year of her father's voluntary imprisonment (83); goes to Sutpen's Hundred in 1864; driven there by Wash Jones; hint of the affair with his grand-daughter is given by Rosa; it is the night that Henry murders Charles Bon (134–35); Clytie tries to stop her from entering (140–42); Rosa confesses that, without having seen Bon but only his picture, she was in love with him at 14 and loved him better than Judith ever could have (144–48); Judith refuses to allow her to see Bon's body (149); she helps carry the coffin (151); she stays at the Hundred waiting for Thomas Sutpen to come home (154); Rosa, Judith, and Clytie live there from the summer of 1865 to January 1866, at which time he returns (158); three months later [April 1866] Rosa is engaged to him (158, 164); another reason for her wearing black for 43 years is shown

(169–170); rejects Sutpen when he insults her (169–72); dies January 8, 1910; buried the next day (173); the affront to her was Sutpen's suggestion that they breed together experimentally, and, if a boy were born, he would marry her (177); she buys and raises Judith's tombstone (211); strikes Clytie down with her fist when she tries to stop her from finding Henry at the Hundred in 1909 (351).

————: French architect who stays two years (1833–35) with Sutpen and directs the bulding of his house (35 & earlier); makes abortive attempt to escape (218).

Goodhue (212) Coldfield (25): Born in Tennessee; arrives in Mississippi in 1828 (381); father of Ellen and Rosa (25); signs a bond for Sutpen when he is arrested (50); dies in 1864 (59); nails himself in attic and starves to death (60, 84); hides from Confederate Provost Marshals for 4 years (68).

———— *Coldfield:* Wife of Goodhue Coldfield, mother of Ellen and Rosa; at least 40 years old when Rosa was born; she dies in 1845 (59).

———— *Coldfield:* Paternal aunt to Ellen and Rosa (25, 50); a spinster who raises Rosa (59); one night she climbs out a window and vanishes (64); she elopes c. 1854 (70) with a horse and mule trader (76).

General (33) [Jason Lycurgus] Compson (12): Grandfather of Quentin III, the closest thing to a friend that Sutpen had on earth (12).

———— *Compson:* Wife of General Compson and grandmother of Quentin III, not a native of Jefferson (54).

———— *Akers:* The man who discovers one of Sutpen's slaves sleeping in the mud (36).

Wash Jones (26): Works for Colonel Sutpen; reports killing of Bon by Henry to Miss Rosa (133); drives her to Sutpen's Hundred in 1864 (134); has one daughter who had an illegitimate daughter who bears Sutpen's child (171–72); his daughter is reported to have died in Memphis brothel (171); Jones dies 12 hours after Sutpen (186); past 60 when he dies (290); when his granddaughter bears a child by Sutpen, he cuts her throat and the infant's throat (291–92); is killed by Major de Spain (292) in 1869 (382).

————: White man who helps Wash Jones build Bon's coffin (150).

Theophilus McCaslin: Attends Bon's funeral and gives Rebel's yell in lieu of a prayer (152).

————: Negro midwife who attends Milly and witnesses Sutpen's murder (185).

Luster: Negro servant of Compson family (187).

————: Female Negro servant of Bon's mistress (193).

Major [Cassius] de Spain: leader of a posse; kills Wash Jones (292).

Melicent Jones: Daughter of Wash Jones; date of birth unknown; rumored to have died in a Memphis brothel (171, 382).

Milly (185) Jones: Wash Jones's illegitimate granddaughter; unmarried mother of Sutpen's daughter (171); murdered—her throat is cut—by her grandfather immediately after the birth (292).

———— *Jones–Sutpen:* Unnamed daughter of Thomas Sutpen; great granddaughter of Wash Jones, who cuts her throat at birth (292).

Judge Benbow: An early friend of Sutpen (46).

Clytie (Clytemnestra) [Sutpen]: Sutpen's illegitimate daughter; half-Negro (61); she should have been named Cassandra, according to Quentin's father (62); aged 74 in 1909 (136), born 1834 (382); buries Judith and pays for the tombstone for Charles Bon's son (210); raises Charles Bon's grandson (210); dies 1910 (382).

Colonel [John] Sartoris: Leads a regiment from Jefferson in 1861 with Sutpen as second in command (80, 121, 124); he is deposed by his officers and Sutpen elected colonel (126).

Charles Bon (67): Born 1829 in Haiti (379); he meets Henry at the University c. 1857–58; his home is New Orleans (70); he is a few years old than Henry; has no parents but a guardian (74); he is engaged to Judith (75); enlists with Henry as a private (87); Bon already has a child whose picture Judith finds on his body (90); he has a nonwhite mistress (92–93); he sees the mistress as no real barrier to the wedding (92); he really loves Judith, but she is not the first to whom he has been pledged (94); his mistress is an octoroon (95); Bon seduced Henry "as surely as he seduced Judith." (96); Henry gives him four years to renounce his mistress (97); there is no actual engagement; he and Judith meet only three times in two years (92); yet Henry has to kill Bon to keep them from marrying (95); Judith buries him herself beside her mother (104); Quentin's father imaginatively reconstructs the scene in which Charles tells Henry of his acquisition of the octoroon (116–18); Bon has not actually seduced Judith (120); he receives a lieutenancy before their first battle (124); is killed by Henry (132–33); dies May 3, 1865, aged 33 years 5 months (134 ff., 190); he is Sutpen's son by his West Indian wife (265); according to Shreve's guess, at the time of the estrangement between Bon and Henry, Bon does not know that he is Judith's brother (296); carries a letter of introduction to Henry from the attorney for his mother; the two meet at the University of Mississippi (313–15); gradually, before he visits the Hundred, he begins to suspect that Henry and he are brothers (318–19); Shreve insists that it is Henry and *not* Bon who is wounded, and that Henry wants Bon to return and marry his own sister; Henry fully agrees to the incest [His ultimate revolt is not against incest, but against miscegenation.]; he wants his father to acknowledge Bon as his son (356 & earlier); if Sutpen does so, Bon will give up all thought of Judith; Bon insists that Henry stop him from marrying Judith by killing him (357).

————: Charles Bon's octoroon mistress (114); brought to Bon's grave with her son in 1870 by Judith (192–93); stays a week (194); dies c. December 1871 (195).

Charles Etienne Saint-Valery (191) Bon (114): The son of Charles Bon by his octoroon mistress; found by Clytie and brought back to Sutpen's Hundred (191); born 1859; died 1884 (191); returns to the Hundred in December 1871 (195); begins to associate with Negroes; gets into a knife fight with Negroes; is arrested (201–02); Quentin's grandfather pays his fine and he leaves the neighborhood (204); returns a year later married to a full-blooded Negro (205); a son is born c. 1881 (205); gets yellow fever; is nursed by Judith who dies first; he dies February 1884 (210–11).

————: Negro wife of Charles E. St.-V. Bon (205).

Jim Bond (214): Son of Charles E. St.-V. Bon (205), born Sutpen's Hundred, 1882 (383); raised by Clytie (210); disappears 1910 (383).

Jim Hamblett: Justice, who tries Charles E. St.-V. Bon (203).

————: Attorney to Charles Bon's mother; planned to blackmail Sutpen (300 ff.) hired for revenge; he deceives Bon's mother to blackmail Sutpen for himself (304–05).

Appendix B:
Notes to *Absalom, Absalom!*

by Cleanth Brooks

What We Know about Thomas Sutpen and His Children

All the information the reader has comes through Quentin directly or through Quentin's conversations with his father, Mr. Compson, and with Miss Rosa Coldfield. The information from General Compson comes to Quentin presumably through Mr. Compson, for though the General did not die until Quentin was ten years old, there is no indication in *Absalom, Absalom!* that the General discussed the matter with his grandson, nor is it likely that he would have done so.

Fact or Event	Ultimate Authority	Page
Sutpen's life in Jefferson from 1833 until 1860.	Gen. Compson and Miss Rosa	p. 8 and passim
Sutpen in 1834 tells Gen. Compson about his early life; stops with his engagement; then waits 30 years to go on with it.	Gen. Compson	pp. 219–58
Bon's friendship with Henry and Judith.	Gen. Compson and Miss Rosa	p. 67 and passim
Charles Bon visits Henry (Christmas, 1859, and summer, 1860).	Gen. Compson	p. 70
Sutpen visits New Orleans summer (or late spring), 1860.	Gen. Compson	p. 70
Henry brings Bon home (Christmas, 1860), quarrels with his father, and leaves home with Bon.	The Negro servants at Sutpen's Hundred (as reported by Gen. Compson).	pp. 78–79

"*Notes to* Absalom, Absalom!" *From* William Faulkner: The Yoknapatawpha Country *by Cleanth Brooks (New Haven: Yale University Press, 1963), pp. 429–36. Copyright © 1963 by Yale University Press. Reprinted by permission of the publisher.*

Fact or Event	Ultimate Authority	Page
Charles Bon and Henry enlist. Bon is soon made a lieutenant.	Gen. Compson	pp. 122–24
Henry and his father meet and talk in Carolina, 1865.	Gen. Compson	p. 276
Bon's letter to Judith in 1865, telling her that he is coming back to marry her.	The letter was preserved by Gen. Compson	pp. 129–32
Judith makes her wedding gown.	Gen. Compson	p. 132
Judith finds on Bon's dead body the picture of the octoroon woman and her child.	Gen. Compson, who presumably learned this from Judith (Miss Rosa probably went to her grave believing that the picture was of Judith).	pp. 90, 95 p. 142
Sutpen returns (autumn, 1864) with the gravestones and tells Gen. Compson about his first marriage and his "design."	Gen. Compson	pp. 188, 270
Sutpen's return from the war (Jan. 1866) and his subsequent life at Sutpen's Hundred.	Miss Rosa and Gen. Compson	p. 158 and passim
Sutpen refuses to join the Ku Klux Klan.	Miss Rosa	p. 161
Sutpen makes his proposal to Miss Rosa.	Miss Rosa	pp. 164–68
Sutpen sets up his little store.	Gen. Compson	p. 180 and passim
Gen. Compson overhears Sutpen and Wash talking about Milly.	Gen. Compson	pp. 283–84
Wash kills Sutpen.	The Negro midwife	pp. 185, 285–88
Wash kills his daughter and is killed.	Gen. Compson	pp. 291–92
Judith buries her father.	Gen. Compson	pp. 185–86
Bon's octoroon mistress visits his grave (summer, 1870).	Gen. Compson	pp. 192–95
Etienne Bon is brought to Sutpen's Hundred (Dec. 1871).	Gen. Compson	p. 195
The piece of mirror is found under Etienne Bon's bed.	Gen. Compson (from information presumably communicated by Judith).	p. 199

Fact or Event	Ultimate Authority	Page
Etienne Bon's indictment.	Gen. Compson	p. 203
Etienne Bon marries.	Gen. Compson	p. 205
Judith nurses Etienne Bon.	Gen. Compson	p. 210
Judith and Etienne die (1884).	Gen. Compson	p. 210
Henry returns to Sutpen's Hundred (1905).	Quentin	p. 373
Quentin learned something on his visit to Sutpen's Hundred (Sept. 1909) which altered his notion of the Sutpen story.	Quentin	p. 373
Clytie sets fire to Sutpen's Hundred; she and Henry die (Dec. 1909).	Mr. Compson	pp. 374–76

What Miss Rosa and General Compson Did Not Know

Miss Rosa did not know that the picture that Judith found on Bon's body was that of his octoroon mistress.	p. 142
Gen Compson did not know that Bon was Henry's part-Negro half-brother.	p. 274
Neither did Miss Rosa know this, unless she learned it at the same time that Quentin did, in Sept. 1909.	p. 18

The More Important Conjectures Made about Thomas Sutpen and His Family

Conjecture	Made by	Page
Sutpen named all his children including Charles Bon.	Gen. Compson	p. 61
	Mr. Compson	pp. 265–66
Miss Rosa hated her father.	Mr. Compson	p. 83
During the war Judith knew where Henry and Bon were.	Mr. Compson	p. 87
Bon must have learned of Sutpen's visit to New Orleans when he himself returned to New Orleans in the summer of 1860.	Mr. Compson	p. 92

Conjecture	_Made by_	_Page_
Sutpen told Henry of Bon's "marriage" to the octoroon woman.	Mr. Compson	p. 90
Bon brought Henry to see the octoroon woman in New Orleans.	Mr. Compson	pp. 108–18
Henry's objection to the marriage of Bon and Judith was the fact that Bon had gone through the ceremony with the octoroon woman.	Mr. Compson	pp. 118–19
Henry and Bon hoped that the war would settle the dispute by removing one of them.	Mr. Compson	p. 120
Judith did not ask her father what his objection was to Bon.	Mr. Compson	p. 120
Henry and Bon returned to Oxford only long enough to enroll in the company being formed at the university.	Mr. Compson	p. 122
Bon was wounded at Shiloh and carried back to safety by Henry.	Mr. Compson (Or does Mr. Compson _know_ this? Shreve questions it on p. 344.)	p. 124
Sutpen's first wife was in New Orleans and Sutpen journeyed there in 1860 to buy her off.	Mr. Compson conjectures this after Quentin had seen Henry. The "Genealogy" printed at the back of the Modern Library edition states that "Eulalia Bon died in New Orleans," and thus provides auctorial sanction for this conjecture. Mr. Compson's first conjecture had been that Sutpen went to New Orleans to check on Bon's octoroon mistress.	pp. 268–69
The conversation between Judith and her father when he returned in 1864.	Quentin	p. 271
At Christmas Sutpen told Henry that Bon was his brother and that Bon knew	Shreve (On p. 303 it is said that Shreve was speaking though "it might have	pp. 293–96

Conjecture	*Made by*	*Page*
this; but Bon did not know it.	been either of them and was in a sense both." But it is clearly Shreve who is speaking from p. 303 to p. 333, from p. 336 to p. 345, from p. 350 to p. 351, and from p. 358 to p. 359. Moreover, save for a dozen or so words, nothing in section 7 is *specifically* assigned to Quentin.)	
There was a lawyer in New Orleans counseling Sutpen's first wife.	Shreve	p. 304
Perhaps Bon's mother discovered that he had an octoroon mistress and child.	Shreve	p. 307
Bon's mother had made the lawyer promise not to tell Bon who his father was.	Shreve	p. 309
The lawyer discovered where Sutpen lived and that Henry attended the University of Mississippi.	Shreve	pp. 309–10
The lawyer wrote to Henry; Henry showed the letter to Bon; and Bon suspected that Henry might be his brother.	Shreve	p. 313
Bon accepted Henry's invitation to visit him, thinking that he might see his father.	Shreve	p. 319
Bon did not know "whatever it was in mother's [blood that Sutpen] could not brook."	Shreve	p. 321
Bon wanted only a hint of recognition from his father; he would not even demand to know "what it was my mother did that justified his action toward her and me." (Shreve evidently assumes at this point that Bon knew nothing of his possession of Negro blood.)	Shreve	p. 327
Bon believed that Sutpen had gone to New Orleans to make	Shreve	p. 329

Conjecture	Made by	Page
sure that Bon was truly his son.		
Bon having returned to New Orleans did not learn whether Sutpen had seen his mother, but continued to believe that he had.	Shreve	p. 331
Sutpen told Henry on the second Christmas visit that Bon was his brother.	Shreve	p. 334
Henry and Bon visited Bon's mother and heard her say "So [Judith] has fallen in love with [Charles]," and Henry "knows" that Bon is indeed his brother.	Shreve ("that drawing room of baroque and fusty magnificence which Shreve had invented and which was probably true enough" and "this slight dowdy woman . . . whom Shreve and Quentin had likewise invented and which was [a construction] likewise probably true enough")	pp. 335–36
The lawyer congratulates Bon and Bon forces an apology.	Shreve	pp. 338–39
In 1862, when Bon was recovering from his wound, he received his octoroon mistress' picture and an appeal for money: she wrote that the lawyer had fled and that she could not find Bon's mother.	Shreve	p. 339
Henry wrestled with his horror of incest and asked Bon: "must you marry [our sister]?"	Shreve	p. 341
Bon did not know what he meant to do though he pretended he did. Henry knew what he meant to do, but had to say that he did not know.	Shreve	p. 341
Henry allowed Bon to write one letter to Judith.	Shreve	p. 342
It was Henry, not Bon, who was wounded at Shiloh.	Shreve	p. 344
In 1864 Bon asked Henry whether he had his permission	Shreve or Quentin?	p. 349

Conjecture	*Made by*	*Page*
to marry Judith, and Henry told him to write to Judith.		
In 1864 Sutpen met Henry and told him that he had seen Charles Bon. (But p. 352 seems to contradict this. Compare also with the conjecture that Bon would have abandoned his courtship of Judith if he had had only a nod of recognition from his father, p. 327.)	Shreve or Quentin?	p. 353
Sutpen also told Henry that Bon's mother was part Negro.	Shreve or Quentin?	pp. 354–55
Bon said to Henry: "So it's the miscegenation, not the incest, which you can't bear." Does this conjecture imply that Henry proceeded to tell Bon what his father had just told him (pp. 354–55)? (As late as p. 327, Quentin and Shreve take for granted that Bon did not know that he had Negro blood.)	Shreve or Quentin?	p. 356
Bon told Henry that mere recognition could have stopped him, but now "I am thinking of myself."	Shreve or Quentin?	p. 357
Bon offered his pistol to Henry, but Henry hurled the pistol away.	Shreve or Quentin?	p. 358
Bon's motive in substituting the picture of his octoroon mistress and child for that of Judith was to say to Judith— if Henry did kill him—"I was no good; do not grieve for me."	Shreve	pp. 358–59

Chronology of Important Dates

	Faulkner	*The Age*
1897	Born (September 25), New Albany, Miss.	McKinley inaugurated as President.
1898		Spanish-American War.
1902	Family moves to Oxford, Miss.	
1914		World War I begins.
1916		James Joyce, *A Portrait of the Artist as a Young Man*.
1917		U.S. enters war.
1918	Joins RAF, trains in Canada.	Armistice signed.
1919	Enrolls as student at University of Mississippi.	Prohibition adopted nationally. Sherwood Anderson, *Winesburg, Ohio*.
1920	Lives in New York City, works as clerk in bookshop.	Warren Harding elected President.
1921	Becomes postmaster at University of Mississippi.	
1922		James Joyce, *Ulysses*. T. S. Eliot, *The Waste Land*. *The Fugitive* (periodical) published.
1924		Ku Klux Klan reborn in South.
1925	Lives in New Orleans. Associates with Sherwood Anderson. Writes *Soldiers' Pay*. Visits Europe. Returns to Oxford, Miss.	Trial in Tennessee of John T. Scopes for teaching Darwin's theory of evolution. F. Scott Fitzgerald, *The Great Gatsby*. Ernest Hemingway, *In Our Time*.
1926	*Soldiers' Pay* published.	Hemingway, *The Sun Also Rises*.

1927	*Mosquitoes.*	
1929	*Sartoris. The Sound and the Fury.* Marries Estelle Oldham.	Thomas Wolfe, *Look Homeward, Angel.* Hemingway, *A Farewell to Arms.* Wall St. crash.
1930	*As I Lay Dying.*	*I'll Take My Stand* by "Twelve Southerners."
1931	*Sanctuary. These Thirteen* (Short Stories).	
1932	Works in Hollywood. *Light in August.*	Franklin Delano Roosevelt elected President.
1933	Daughter Jill born. *A Green Bough* (Poems).	Prohibition ends.
1934	*Dr. Martino and Other Stories.*	Fitzgerald, *Tender Is the Night.*
1935	Brother Dean killed piloting Faulkner's plane. *Pylon.*	
1936	*Absalom, Absalom!.*	Civil War in Spain.
1938	*The Unvanquished.*	Allen Tate, *The Fathers.*
1939	*The Wild Palms.*	World War II begins.
1940	*The Hamlet.*	Hemingway, *For Whom the Bell Tolls.* End of "phony war." France falls.
1941		U.S. enters war.
1942	*Go Down, Moses.* Works in Hollywood.	
1945		Truman becomes President on Roosevelt's death. Atomic bombs dropped on Japan. World War II ends.
1946	Malcolm Cowley edits and publishes *The Portable Faulkner.*	Beginning of Cold War.
1948	*Intruder in the Dust.*	
1949	*Knight's Gambit.*	
1950	*Collected Stories.* Awarded Nobel Prize for Literature.	
1951	*Requiem for a Nun.*	
1954	*A Fable.*	Supreme Court school desegregation decision.

1955	National Book Award, Pulitzer Prize.	
1957	*The Town.* Writer in residence, University of Virginia.	
1958		Montgomery, Ala., civil rights protest.
1959	*The Mansion.*	
1962	*The Reivers.* Dies (July 6).	Albany, Ga., civil rights protest.

Notes on the Editor and Contributors

ARNOLD GOLDMAN, editor of this volume, is Reader in English and American literature at the University of Sussex. He is the author of *The Joyce Paradox* (1966). Other publications include articles on O'Neill, Dos Passos, and Faulkner.

MELVIN BACKMAN is Professor of English at C. W. Post College of Long Island University. In addition to various articles on Faulkner he has written about Hemingway.

CLEANTH BROOKS is Professor of English at Yale University. A prominent force in the movement known as "the New Criticism," his books include *Modern Poetry and the Tradition* (1939), *The Well Wrought Urn* (1947), *Literary Criticism: A Short History* (1957, with W. K. Wimsatt), *The Hidden God: Studies in Hemingway, Faulkner, Yeats, Eliot, and Warren* (1963), and *A Shaping Joy: Studies in the Writer's Craft* (1971).

THOMAS E. CONNOLLY teaches at the State University of New York at Buffalo. He is the author of three books on James Joyce, including his edition of *Scribbledehobble* (1961), a book on Swinburne, and articles on Hawthorne, Pound, Keats, and Dickens.

JAMES GUETTI's book *The Limits of Metaphor* is a study of Melville, Conrad, and Faulkner. He is Associate Professor of English at Rutgers, the State University of New Jersey, where he teaches a course in Rhetoric and Literary Form.

MICHAEL MILLGATE, after teaching English and American literature at the University of Leeds, moved to Canada, teaching first at York University, Toronto, and presently at the University of Toronto. Besides two books on Faulkner and an edition of interviews with Faulkner, *Lion in the Garden* (1968, with James Meriwether), he is the author of *American Social Fiction: James to Cozzens* (1964) and *Thomas Hardy: His Career as a Novelist* (1971).

JOHN PATERSON is the author of *The Making of "The Return of the Native"* (Berkeley: University of California Press, 1960) and the editor of the Riverside edition of George Eliot's *Adam Bede*. He is an Associate Professor at the University of California, Berkeley.

RICHARD POIRIER wrote his essay on *Absalom, Absalom!* when in his early twenties. He is presently chairman of the Humanities at Rutgers, and an editor of *Partisan Review*. He is the author of *The Comic Sense of Henry James* (1960); *A World Elsewhere* (1966), a study of American literature; and *The Performing Self* (1971).

Selected Bibliography

Adams, Richard P., *Faulkner: Myth and Motion* (Princeton, N.J.: Princeton University Press, 1968), pp. 172–214. The novel "is finally not so much historiographical as mythical," proceeding from "Miss Rosa's gothic tale" to "Mr. Compson's tragic version" to other "more complex" interpretations, but "the circumstances of life, change, and motion . . . overwhelm the static design."

Brooks, Cleanth, *William Faulkner: The Yoknapatawpha Country* (New Haven and London: Yale University Press, 1963), pp. 295–324. Reprinted in *Faulkner: A Collection of Critical Essays*, ed. Robert Penn Warren (Englewood Cliffs, N.J.: Prentice-Hall, Inc., 1966), pp. 186–203. A close reading of the text, with an emphasis on Thomas Sutpen's "Americanness."

Howe, Irving, *William Faulkner: A Critical Study*, revised edition (New York: Vintage Books, 1962), pp. 71–78. A good statement of the novel's gothic qualities.

Langford, Gerald, *Faulkner's Revision of "Absalom, Absalom!": A Collection of the Manuscript and the Published Book* (Austin: University of Texas Press, 1971).

Lind, Ilse Dusoir, "The Design and Meaning of *Absalom, Absalom!*," *PMLA* 60 (December, 1955): 887–912. Reprinted in *William Faulkner: Three Decades of Criticism*, eds. Frederick J. Hoffman and Olga W. Vickery (East Lansing: Michigan State University Press, 1960; New York: Harbinger Books, 1963), pp. 278–304.

Sewall, Richard B., *The Vision of Tragedy* (New Haven and London: Yale University Press, 1959), pp. 133–47. "The tragedy is Quentin's:" "this full and tragic realization . . . of the paradox of his Southern heritage . . . with which he must somehow come to terms and cannot."

Swiggart, Peter, *The Art of Faulkner's Novels* (Austin: University of Texas Press, 1962), pp. 149–70. *Absalom, Absalom!* is "A Puritan Tragedy": Sutpen is "an allegorical representative of the South's puritan aristocracy. The essay attempts to relate "the Sutpen tragedy and the South's moral failure," seeing "a conflict between two conceptions of human dignity" as "underlying" the novel.

Thompson, Lawrance, *William Faulkner* (New York: Barnes and Noble, 1963), pp. 53–65. The novel's relation to Greek myth and Bible story is examined.

Vickery, Olga W., *The Novels of William Faulkner: A Critical Interpretation*, rev. ed. (Baton Rouge: Louisiana State University Press, 1964), pp. 84–102.

Waggoner, Hyatt H., *William Faulkner: From Jefferson to the World* (Lexington: University of Kentucky Press, 1959), pp. 148–69. Reprinted in Warren, ed. *Faulkner, A Collection of Critical Essays*, pp. 175–85. This essay is particularly interesting on the structure of "frames" through which the story of Sutpen is told.

Zoellner, Robert H., "Faulkner's Prose Style in *Absalom, Absalom!*," *American Literature* 30 (1958–59): 486–502. Close stylistic analyses of specimen passages lead to a description of "characteristically Faulknerian" rhetorical devices: syntactical ambiguity, time alternation, delayed modification, suspension and enclosure, and dramatic periodicity. These are related to the meaning of the novel and to "the philosophical conviction, that life is in all its aspects a continuum that cannot be compartmentalized without substantial loss of truth."

TWENTIETH CENTURY
INTERPRETATIONS

MAYNARD MACK, *Series Editor*
Yale University

NOW AVAILABLE
Collections of Critical Essays
ON

(continued on next page)

(continued from previous page)

JULIUS CAESAR
KEATS'S ODES
LIGHT IN AUGUST
LORD JIM
MAJOR BARBARA
MEASURE FOR MEASURE
THE MERCHANT OF VENICE
MISS LONELYHEARTS
MOLLOY, MALONE DIES, THE UNNAMABLE
MOLL FLANDERS
MUCH ADO ABOUT NOTHING
MURDER IN THE CATHEDRAL
THE NIGGER OF THE "NARCISSUS"
1984
OEDIPUS REX
THE OLD MAN AND THE SEA
PAMELA
A PASSAGE TO INDIA
THE PLAYBOY OF THE WESTERN WORLD
THE PORTRAIT OF A LADY
A PORTRAIT OF THE ARTIST AS A YOUNG MAN
THE PRAISE OF FOLLY
PRIDE AND PREJUDICE
THE RAINBOW
THE RAPE OF THE LOCK
RICHARD II
THE RIME OF THE ANCIENT MARINER
ROBINSON CRUSOE
ROMEO AND JULIET
SAMSON AGONISTES
THE SCARLET LETTER
SIR GAWAIN AND THE GREEN KNIGHT
SONGS OF INNOCENCE AND OF EXPERIENCE
SONS AND LOVERS
THE SOUND AND THE FURY
A STREETCAR NAMED DESIRE
THE TEMPEST
TESS OF THE D'URBERVILLES
TOM JONES
TO THE LIGHTHOUSE
THE TURN OF THE SCREW AND OTHER TALES
TWELFTH NIGHT
UTOPIA
VANITY FAIR
WALDEN
THE WASTE LAND
WOMEN IN LOVE
WUTHERING HEIGHTS